Cyprus

YPT

SUDAN

Perim I.

BRITISH
SOMALILAND

BRITISH
ST AFRICA

Zanzibar

ODESIA

UTH
ICA

Mauritius

Laccadives

Maldives

Ceylon

Seychelles

Chagos Is.

Cocos Is.

INDIA

Andaman Is.

Nicobar Is.

BURMA

Hong Kong

FEDERAL
MALAY
STATES

BORNEO

Christmas I.

NEW GUINEA

COMMONWEALTH
of AUSTRALIA

TASMANIA

Solomon Is.

Ellice Is.

Fiji Is.

Norfolk I.

DOMINION of NEW ZEALAND

The British Empire, circa 1900.

First published 1974
Third reprint 1979
Macdonald Educational Ltd
Holywell House, Worship Street
London EC2A 2EN
© Macdonald Educational
Limited 1974

Printed in England by
Hazell Watson & Viney Ltd
Aylesbury, Bucks

Edited by Sue Jacquemier
Research: Bridget Hadaway
Assistant Editor: Tim Healey

ISBN 0 356 04453 X
Library of Congress Catalog Card
Number: 73-172433

We wish to thank the following individuals and organizations for their assistance and for making available material in their collections.

American Embassy, London: A. C. Cooper *page 64(R)*
American Heritage:
   (Chicago Historical Society) *page 72*
   (Fine Arts Collection, Seaman's Bank for Savings) *page 56(L) (TR)*
   (Gettysburg National Military Park) *page 74*
   (The Old Print Shop) *page 73(TL)*
   (Peabody Museum, Salem, Massachusetts) *page 73(TR)*
   (Wadsworth Athenean) *page 73(B)*
Amon Carter Museum, Fort Worth, Texas *page 77(T)*
Andrew Mollo Collection: Chris Barker *pages 66(TL), 66–67(B)*
Angelo Hornak *page 23(TL)*
T. & R. Annan & Sons *page 82(L)*
Anne S. K. Brown Military Collection *pages 59(BL), 71(T)*
Balmer, Derek *pages 57(B), 59(T), 61(C)*
Barker, Chris *page 21(B)*
Bettmann Archive *pages 61(TR) (B), 63(CL), 67(BR), 81(T)*
Brinson, David *page 9(CL)*
Bristol Royal Agricultural Society: John Webb *page 25(TR)*
Broadlands Collection *page 19(B)*
Camden Libraries & Arts Department: K. Hoddle *page 40(BR)*
Camera Press *page 61(TC)*
Chicago Historical Society *page 75(BR)*
Collection A. Francombe *page 9(BR)*
Communist Party Library: Chris Barker *pages 30–31(B)*

Confederate High Command: U.K. division: *page 65(CR)*
Crown copyright: *pages 5(B), 11(T), 85(BR)*
   Victoria and Albert Museum *page 43(TR)*
   Angelo Hornak *page 66(BL)*
Culff, Robert: A. C. Cooper *page 41(TL)*
De La Rue Company Limited: K. Hoddle *page 13(CL)*
Dickens House *page 35(CL)*
Dixson Library, Sydney *page 81(CR)*
Edwards, Francis *page 7(BR)*
Freeman, John *page 31(TC)*
George Eastman House: Lewis Hine *page 35(TL)*
Gibbons, Stanley *pages 50(T), 65(CL)*
Gilbert, Martin *page 52(L)*
G.L.C. Record Office: Nightingale Collection *page 37(B)*
   Sue Gooders *page 5(T)*
Godden, Geoffrey *page 15(TL), (B)*
Guildhall Library: Sue Gooders *pages 7(CR), 9(CR) (BL), 15(CR), 41(BL) (BC) (BR), 46(CL), 47(C)*
Hall, Jeremy *page 70(T), 76(TR)*
Hoddle, K. *page 18(T), 41(TR)*
Hulton Picture Library *pages 8(CL), 10(R), 12(R), 13(B), 17(TL) (BR), 19(T), 22(L), 24(L), 25(CR), 26(T), 27(CL), 35(BR), 37(TR), 39(BR), 44(L), 49(B), 53(B), 60, 61(TL), 67(TL), 83(T), 85(TL)*
Hunstein, Don *page 21(TR)*
Huskison, Tony *page 8(CR)*
Illustrated London News *page 35(TR)*
India Office Library: R. B. Fleming *pages 53(T) (C), 56(BR)*
Kansas State Historical Society *page 79(CL)*
Kean Archives *page 75(TL)*
Kodak Museum *page 13(TL)*
Leighton House *page 11(B)*
Library of Congress *pages 14(TR), 37(TL), 63(CR), 70(BL), 71(B), 77(BR), 79(TL) (BL), 81(BR)*
L'illustration *page 7(BL)*
London Museum *pages 17(BL), 21(CL), 55(TR)*
Louisiana State Museum *page 62*
Manchester City Art Gallery *page 2(B)*
Mansell Collection *pages 14(BR), 20(TR), 22(R), 24(R), 25(CL) (BL), 31(TL), 32, 34(BL) (R), 37(C), 39(TL) (TR), 41(C), 42(BL), 45(CR), 46(TL), 49(TR), 54(BL), 55(TL), 63(BC), 79(TR), 84(TL) (BL)*
Mary Evans Picture Library *pages 4(L), 10(TL), 14(L), 17(TR), 18(BR), 34(TL), 36(L), 40(L)*
Mary Hillier Collection: A. C. Cooper *page 10(BL)*

Mayer, Francis G. *page 80(L)*
Mitchell Library *page 47(TR)*
Morrison, George *page 45(BL) (CL)*
National Army Museum *pages 50, 85(C) (BR)*
National Buildings Record *page 21(CR)*
National Gallery *page 28*
National Library of Australia: Rex Kivell Collection *pages 46–47, 49(TL) (CR)*
National Maritime Museum *page 26(R)*
National Portrait Gallery *pages 20(BR), 23(CR), 26(B), 42(TR) (BR) (BC) (TL), 44(R), 45(TL)*
New York Historical Society *page 63(T)*
P. & O. Lines *page 7(CR)*
Paul Popper *page 21(TL)*
Pennsylvania Academy of Fine Arts *page 59(CR)*
Press Association *page 12(BL)*
Punch *page 25(TL)*
Purnell S. Africa *page 85(TR)*
Rainbird Publishing *page 27(CR) (BL) (BR)*
Rensselaer Polytechnic Institute *page 69(T)*
R.I.B.A. *page 4(R), 9(T)*
Rudisill, Dick *page 76(L)*
Science Museum, London *pages 8(B), 18(BL), 43(TL)*
Stuart Bale Limited *page 24(TR)*
State Historical Society of Colorado, Denver *page 76(RB)*
Tate Gallery *page 29(BR) (T)*
   John Webb *page 29(BL)*
Trustees of the British Museum *pages 6(B), 20(L), 25(BR)*
   John Webb *pages 16, 55(B), 82(TR)*
   John Freeman *pages 38, 49(CL)*
   Chris Barker *page 65(BL)*
T.U.C.: Chris Barker *page 33*
U.S.I.S. *page 12(TL)*
Victoria and Albert Museum *pages 15(TL), 23(B), 54(TL), 57(T)*
   A. C. Cooper *page 23(TR)*
Viollet, Roger *page 13(BR)*
Walker Art Gallery *page 82(BR)*

Title page (opposite): *(TL)* Confederate flags of the American Civil War (Confederate High Command, U.K. Division).
(BL) Hammer for beating steel (Foto Krupp, Essen).
(TR) Indians surround a wagon train (James Jerome Hill Reference Library).
(BR) American mincing machine of the 1890's (Library of Congress).

Macdonald
Educational

R J Unstead

Age of Machines

A Pictorial History
1815-1901

Volume Seven

The period between 1816 and 1901 saw such an astonishing increase in the use of machinery that it can be fairly called an Age of Machines. Industry, agriculture and transport were transformed. Though many of the inventions and discoveries had been made earlier, the rate of change in the 19th century was unheard of.

The use of coal increased; more coal meant more iron and more iron meant more machines. A cheap steel-making process, invented by Henry Bessemer, led to the production of more sophisticated machinery. Towns and cities increased in size to house the people who worked the machines. The great populations of the towns could now be fed on a larger scale, for agricultural machinery enabled farmers, especially in America, to produce food in hitherto unbelievable quantities. Railways and steamships carried the food and manufactured goods to the world, achieving a revolution in transport.

Industrialization had profound social and political consequences. In the vast towns and factories, men found it easier to band together to protect themselves, demanding reforms in education, housing, health, and working conditions. Industrialization also caused many thinkers and artists to react against a society dominated by machines. For although it might be thought that increased wealth led to greater goodwill and understanding, the sad truth is that the Age of Machines gave man new opportunities to exercise his greed and aggression.

Work, a painting by Ford Madox Brown. Hard work was a Victorian ideal. Here we see six heroic navvies. To left and right, are those who live on the workers' labour—a beggar, gentlefolk and two intelléctuals.

R J Unstead

Age of Machines

In this volume we have tried to show some of the main events, ideas and movements of the English-speaking world in the 19th century.

Here are the advances in transport, trade, industry and farming that made it such a tumultuous period. We also show scenes from everyday life, with the sharp contrast between wealth and poverty. This panorama of society in the days of Dickens and Mark Twain, includes inventors, artists and writers, cowboys and Indians, children and sportsmen. For although this was an Age of Machines, it was also a period on which ordinary and extraordinary people made their mark.

The picture also shows the growth of the British Empire, Ireland's plight, war and crime. Naturally, the United States looms large. In its colossal expansion, in the drama and tragedy of its Civil War and in its emergence as the richest nation on earth, it was the marvel of the century.

Contents

The New Age

When peace came to Europe in 1815, Napoleon was put out of harm's way. France again had a monarch, and the statesmen of Europe met at Vienna to arrange a peace settlement.

Metternich, the Austrian leader, took the lead in trying to ensure that an upheaval like the French Revolution should never again overturn society. The Emperors of Russia and Austria and the King of Prussia formed a "Holy Alliance" to maintain the old order, and to intervene wherever revolution threatened. The British representatives, Castlereagh and Wellington, however, were not enthusiastic about interfering with the domestic affairs of independent states.

Yet, in Britain itself, the government showed no such liberal spirit. Peace had brought renewed hardship for the poor, dear bread, heavy taxation and a temporary decline in trade. The ruling class was still haunted by fear of revolution, and took steps to suppress agitation for parliamentary reform and social justice. The country was about to enter an era of unprecedented prosperity, but, for the time being, the scene was clouded by widespread suffering and discontent.

An anti-Corn Laws riot outside the House of Commons in 1815. During the war when it was impossible to import foreign corn, farmers had been encouraged to grow more wheat. Many had borrowed money to expand their farms. When peace came, they faced ruin for foreign corn was cheaper than their own.

Parliament was dominated by great landlords whose incomes came from tenant farmers and passed a Corn Law putting a tax on foreign corn. The price of home-grown wheat was kept high. Bread, the staple food of the poor, remained expensive for many years.

Right: contrast to the hard lot of the poor, the Banqueting Room in Brighton Pavilion.

The Peterloo Massacre

Since Parliament represented only the upper classes, a number of persons known as "Radicals" felt that political reform must come through a new parliamentary system. When Henry Hunt, a famous Radical orator, was billed to address a meeting in St Peter's Fields, Manchester, local yeomanry were sent to arrest him.

There was jostling and confusion in the huge crowd, whereupon regular cavalry were ordered to charge. Eleven persons were killed and hundreds injured. The government then passed the Six Acts to repress "seditious meetings" and free speech.

The "Peterloo Massacre", 1819.

Table showing how Queen Victoria came to the throne. George III's unattractive sons followed the family tradition of marrying German princesses but they failed to produce a single male heir.

George IV, who had acted as Regent during his father's bouts of insanity, had one daughter, Charlotte, but she died in 1817. William IV, "Sailor Billy", left no children, so the succession fell upon Princess Victoria, eighteen-year-old daughter of the fourth son, Edward, Duke of Kent.

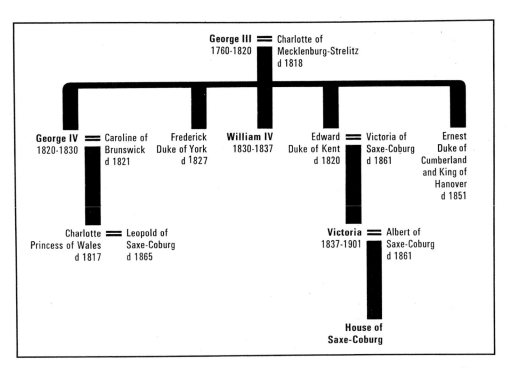

The young Queen Victoria out riding with her Prime Minister, Lord Melbourne, whom she adored. Melbourne, a witty easy-going aristocrat, became friend and counsellor to the inexperienced girl, teaching her the duties of a monarch with tactful charm. He guided Victoria until she married Prince Albert in 1840.

The Duke of Wellington was another trusted adviser. He admired the young Queen's composure. When her reign began, seeing that trade was picking up and public discontent subsiding, he remarked, "Yes, I consider the country is on its legs again".

The Empire-Builders

When the Napoleonic Wars ended, Britain was the only colonial power of any consequence. Yet she made little attempt to add to her overseas possessions. Colonies were felt to be costly luxuries, so Britain declined gains she might have made and merely held on to territories like the Cape of Good Hope, Mauritius, Malta and the Caribbean islands of St Lucia, Trinidad and Tobago. These helped the twin causes of trade and sea-power and enabled the navy to protect colonies which Britain already held.

For this was a trading rather than a ruling empire. In the 1850's, having learned from earlier mistakes, Britain handed out self-government to the Australian colonies, New Zealand and most of the colonies of British North America. India and the East were different for these were the most profitable areas in the world. The East India Company steadily extended British rule in India until the outbreak of the Mutiny in 1857. James Brooke introduced peace and justice into Sarawak, Stamford Raffles founded Singapore and British merchants pushed aggressively into China.

Durbar (ceremonial meeting) at Lahore 1846, when a British officer, Henry Lawrence, was made protective ruler of the Sikh state of the Punjab. The Sikhs had attacked the British and been defeated; in 1848, they rose in revolt and were again defeated, whereupon Dalhousie annexed the whole of the Punjab. Lawrence made it into a model province and the Sikhs stood by the British during the Mutiny of 1857.

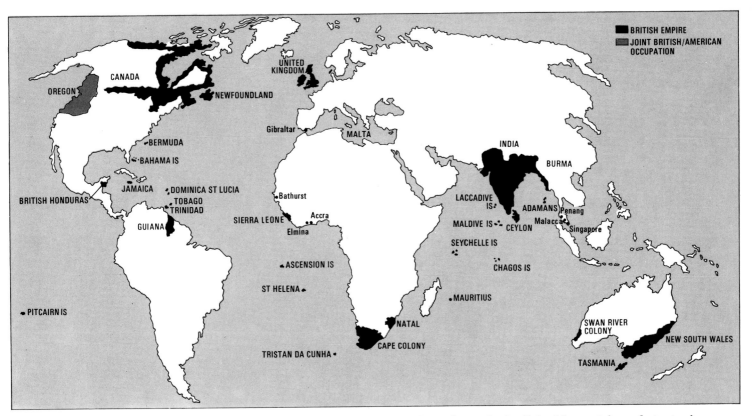

The British Empire 1830 (compare its extent with the map at the front of this book). It already spans the world from Canada to Australasia, linked by a string of strategic bases.

The clipper *Orient* (built 1853) on her way to England with a cargo of Australian wool. Trade links were almost exclusively with Britain, the colonies importing manufactured goods in return for wool, timber and wheat.

An emigrant ship about to leave port in the 1850's. Thousands of Britons settled in Canada and Australasia.

Left: Englishwoman surveys women of the Sudan which Britain came to rule by the end of the century. The empire-builders felt that they were bringing progress and Christianity to backward peoples.

Right: Englishman at breakfast in British India. Middle-class youngsters found a luxurious way of life that often led to affluent retirement. They came to trade or rule, not to settle, as in the "white" colonies.

The Coming of the Railways

In 1825, three of George Stephenson's locomotives ran along the track he had built between Stockton and Darlington. This was the world's first public passenger-carrying railway. It combined steam-engines with horse-drawn coaches: the Liverpool–Manchester line of 1830 was the first to use steam alone. There followed the Great Western and the London–Birmingham–Preston lines, as the first railway boom of the 1830's brought 5,000 miles of railway into operation.

"Railway Mania" gripped the public during the next decade. George Hudson, the "Railway King", and hundreds of others made fortunes or ruined themselves in financing new companies. Stephenson and his son Robert built most of the lines, with Brunel acting as maestro of the Great Western. The actual work of building the tracks, tunnels, bridges and embankments was carried out at amazing speed by a labour force of 200,000 tough, hard-drinking "navvies". By 1870, they had built a network of over 13,000 miles, covering the length and breadth of Britain and revolutionizing the transport of passengers, food, freight and mail.

A railway ticket for the Leicester and Swannington Railway, 1832. From 1844, third-class tickets cost a penny a mile and this meant that all but the poorest could travel about the country for business, pleasure and holidays.

Left: the *Northumbrian* which led the procession at the opening of the Liverpool–Manchester Railway, 1830. Stephenson's *Blucher* had been an improved version of William Hedley's *Puffing Billy* (1813). Next came *Locomotion* (1825) and the famous *Rocket* which won the Rainhill Trials in 1829.

Right: *North Star*, designed by George Stephenson in 1837 for the Great Western Railway. At Killingworth Colliery, the gauge, or distance between rails, had been 4ft 8½ins (1·4m), so Stephenson built *Blucher* to fit this track. Afterwards he always used this gauge for his railways. Brunel, however, preferred a 7ft (2·1m) gauge for the G.W.R. Parliament had to decree that all lines must use Stephenson's 4ft 8½ins gauge—except the G.W.R.!

The Railway Station by William Frith, 1862, which expresses Victorian pride in the railways.

One of the new railways that angered many a landowner.

Right: a driver, one of the new army of railway workers.

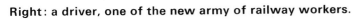

Left: Kilsby Tunnel 1837: flooding was a serious problem.

Below: trestle-bridge, Pacific Railway in America.

Family Life

Inspired by the Royal example and mindful, perhaps, of the seething masses beneath their social level, middle-class Victorians came to regard the family as a sacred unit.

Papa stood at its head, an awesome figure whose word was law to his wife, children and servants. He did not usually marry early; a man was expected to provide a fully furnished home for his bride, and to be well established in life.

His wife usually brought a dowry with her and, on marriage, all her property became her husband's. Their children arrived at regular intervals; there were often ten, twelve or more, for birth-control was practically unknown. Sons were sent to boarding-school and perhaps to university; daughters were educated at home by governesses and later sent to finishing school. As a rule, they had no training for a career but remained at home under Mama's wing, helping to bring up the younger children.

Servants formed an essential part of the household; they attended family prayers, lived below stairs and slept in the attics. They often remained with the same family all their working lives.

Going to church, behaving at meals, addressing an elder, paying calls and receiving guests were all done according to rules. Discipline was strict, and there was a certain amount of tyranny and hypocrisy. Yet, at its best, the life of a Victorian family contained a great deal of fun and affection.

The benevolent Victorian father: his well-behaved children, the youngest carried by the family nannie, troop into his study to say goodnight.

Left: Games played an important part in family life before the days of radio and television. This is a box for the repulsion bell, a toy which gave a score to each player according to luck or skill.

Favourite indoor games included ludo, halma, happy families, alphabet building-blocks, model theatres, jigsaw puzzles, solitaire, toy soldiers and forts.

Above: a Victorian family group of grandparents, parents, maiden aunts and children. Every photograph album contained groups like this one—the large closely-knit family was felt to be the corner-stone of society.

Victorian children often had no friends outside the family, since there were usually sufficient brothers, sisters and cousins to keep them company.

Left: Queen Victoria, Prince Albert and some of their children (they had nine altogether) in 1846.

The Royal couple set an example of family life to a country which had jeered at the low morals of Victoria's uncles. She adored Albert and was grief-stricken by his death. She scarcely appeared in public for ten years and wore black for the rest of her life.

Below: *Conversation Piece* by Joseph Solomon, 1884, a Victorian drawing-room scene where, after dinner, the family and guests divert themselves with music and conversation.

Notice the profusion of ornaments, knick-knacks and plants, the heavy furnishings, the ladies' flounced skirts, slender waists and bustles. The couple are looking at pictures in an album and the maid in cap and apron is adjusting an oil lamp.

Inventions and Daily Life

Our Victorian forefathers were indefatigable inventors. Nearly all of the inventions that we use in everyday life date from their period, though few were widely available until this century. They include the typewriter (1867), the telephone (1876), the phonograph or gramophone (1877), the electric light bulb (1879), photography and, before the end of the century, the motor-car, the electric train, X-rays, the cinema, wireless, celluloid, central-heating and air-conditioning. During Victoria's reign, many familiar electric appliances had already appeared; vacuum-cleaners, floor-polishers, hot-plates, kettles, washing-machines and dish-washers. For farmers there was even an electric milking-machine.

In the middle of the century, road transport still depended largely on the horse. Yet Benz and Daimler were already working on the "horseless carriage" that was to astonish the world in the 1880's. The 1890's saw car production established and Mr Ford in business in Detroit. Meanwhile, the bicycle provided millions with cheap transport. Lilienthal pioneered gliding in sailplanes. Airships relying on steam or electricity proved of little value, but engineers were already experimenting with other forms of powered flight.

From about 1860, the Bessemer and Siemens-Martin processes produced cast steel in great quantity for ships, and also for great structures like the Brooklyn and Forth bridges. The first effective submarines appeared, and so did dynamite, land-mines and machine-guns. There was a host of lesser inventions, from moving staircases, electric fans and hydraulic lifts, to slot-machines, shower-baths, and talking dolls.

The Morse telegraph devised by Samuel Morse in about 1844.

Engraving of Reuter's pigeon-post service, 1850. Paul Reuter, a German, turned next to the electric telegraph and set up a world-wide news agency in London.

New electric lighting flooding the Mansion House and the Royal Exchange in London, in 1881.

Electricity was the new miracle power; the 1830's saw the birth of primitive dynamos, electric motors and the electro-magnetic telegraph. By 1865, generators were available but did not come into wide use until

Edison's incandescent lamp (1879) led to the introduction of power stations. These promoted the use of electric motors in trams and trains, as well as the electric lighting of some streets and homes.

Widespread use of electricity in industry did not develop until the 20th century.

Left: a typical bellows-camera of the 1880's. Cameras developed from the *camera obscura*, a darkened box which caused images of an object to appear on a white surface.

In 1837, Daguerre, a Frenchman, made this image permanent by using an iodized silver plate; then, in about 1840, came Fox-Talbot's process, using a chemically treated paper.

By the late 1850's, photography had become a popular medium for family portraits.

De La Rue's patent envelope machine at the Great Exhibition where Victorian inventors were able to display their ingenuity to the public.

Thomas Alva Edison, the American genius who played a prominent part in developing the electric light bulb, telephone, microphone, gramophone and cinematograph.

He founded a company to make incandescent lights with an Englishman, Joseph Swann. He improved Bell's telephone by using a carbon microphone, patented a gramophone in 1877 and, a few years later, developed a high-speed camera for motion pictures.

At one time, he was working on no fewer than 45 inventions.

Right: the Penny Black, first issued 6 May 1840. Prior to 1830, letters were carried by horse-drawn mail-coaches. Then the railways brought a speedier and more reliable service.

The cost of sending a letter depended upon its weight and the distance it had to travel, so all kinds of dodges were used to cheat the Post Office.

In 1840, Rowland Hill's scheme for a Penny Post was introduced for all letters under half an ounce in weight.

Sport and Leisure

More than ever before, people began to seek pleasure outside their own homes and towns. Railways and newspapers helped to widen their horizons and to make them interested in places and events beyond their neighbourhoods.

The Prince Regent had made Brighton popular and there were now dozens of seaside resorts to which people could make day trips or take a holiday in one of the new hotels or boarding-houses. Sport began to be organized on a national level, as modern soccer and rugby emerged; cricket was the aristocrat of games, while tennis and golf started to appeal to a wider public. Amateurs fully held their own, especially in cricket and football, where teams like the Old Etonians and Corinthians were a match for professional sides.

It was a great age for the theatre, with actor-managers like Irving and Tree putting on plays by Barrie, Oscar Wilde and Bernard Shaw for star performers such as Ellen Terry, Charles Hawtrey and Mrs Patrick Campbell. The music-halls with their robust humour, their patriotic and sentimental songs, held a tremendous fascination for all classes.

Genteel pastime for a young lady. At her finishing school she would have learnt painting, drawing, playing the piano, needlework and flower-arrangement.

Above right: cover for *Harper's*, an American monthly magazine. Popular journals included *Blackwood's Magazine*, the *Illustrated London News*, and the *Boy's Own Paper*.

Right: a party of Thomas Cook's tourists about to visit the pyramids in Egypt. Cook began organizing excursions in 1841 when railways made cheap travel possible. By the 1860's, he was organizing trips to the U.S., Palestine, Italy and Egypt.

14

At the theatre: every sizeable town had a thriving theatre and at least one music-hall. The vast Albert Hall in London was opened in 1871.

A view of the Crystal Palace across the Serpentine in Hyde Park, where the Great Exhibition of 1851 drew over six million visitors. Local councils were now beginning to lay out ornamental gardens and parks.

Left: W. G. Grace, the Grand Old Man of cricket. In his career, he made 126 centuries and took 2,864 wickets.

Below: a woven silk picture of 1881 called *The First Set*. Tennis became popular as a game in which ladies could take part.

The Transport Revolution

The most dramatic development in transport was the growth of the railways. Until the 1830's, every long-distance journey had to be made by stage-coach, private carriage or carrier's cart and a great industry had grown up along McAdam's new roads. Suddenly, it collapsed and the roads were left empty until the arrival of the motor-car.

Town traffic was still horse-drawn. Besides omnibuses, hackney cabs, carts and carriages of every kind, there was also a smart little vehicle, the hansom, which served as the taxi of the period. Horse-drawn trams, introduced in 1861, were followed by steam trams, with electric power in use from 1884. Traffic congestion led to the building of London's underground railway and, by 1900, there were three electric companies in operation.

Bicycles provided a cheap and rapid means of transport and the first motor-cycle appeared in the 1890's. By this time, keen interest had been aroused in the motor-car. Traffic laws hampered its development in Britain until 1896 when, to celebrate the new freedom, a fleet of "horseless carriages" set off from London to Brighton.

A stage-coach at the toll-gate in 1829, the year when the Rainhill Trials demonstrated the efficiency of railways. In a decade or so, they were to force the stage-coaches out of business.

Bicycle advertisement, 1897. The "boneshaker", with wooden wheels and iron tyres, appeared in 1868; then came the "penny-farthing", which had a huge front wheel and pedals fixed to the front hub.

"Stanley's safety bicycle", with equal-sized wheels and chain drive came on the market in 1885. Pneumatic rubber tyres were introduced in 1888.

Mr Gladstone is among the passengers on this trial run of London's first underground railway, the Metropolitan Line, opened in 1862. Steam-engines were used until electric trains arrived in 1890.

Traffic congestion in the city of London, 1872. Apart from bicycles, every vehicle was horse-drawn.

The streets throbbed with the clatter of iron-shod wheels on cobbles, and stank with the smell of horse-droppings. In the city centres, cleaners continually swept them away and children earned a living sweeping crossings for pedestrians and holding the bridles of waiting horses.

Inside a London horse-omnibus. Victorian buses were painted red, green, blue, chocolate, yellow and white according to their routes. They were single-deckers until the Great Exhibition, when so many visitors came to London that the companies put passengers on the roof.

Industry and Trade

Britain's claim to be known as "the workshop of the world" was fully justified in the third quarter of the 19th century. Her ability to supply the world with manufactured goods rested on a combination of skill and luck. In addition to industrial know-how and some brilliant inventors, Britain possessed adequate supplies of coal and plentiful labour. She also had a stable system of government and a large merchant fleet to carry goods all over the world.

The troubled state of potential rivals added to these advantages. America suffered a disastrous civil war, Germany and Italy were struggling for national unity and France experienced the rise and fall of the Second Empire. These distractions delayed industrial progress in countries which might otherwise have overtaken Britain's lead. In 1870, the volume of Britain's trade was more than that of Germany, France and Italy put together and was three or four times that of the U.S. Imports certainly exceeded exports, but the difference was paid for by money that Britain received from interest on foreign loans, shipping, banking and insurance.

Coventry ribbon, woven for the Great Exhibition. It cost 15s. a yard.

Colliery on the Durham coalfield.

Labour yard in London: the poor are employed in breaking stones.

Left: the railway works at Crewe in about 1849. Britain was the first country to build a railway network. Besides supplying her own needs, she was able to export rolling-stock, locomotives and engineers to construct railway systems abroad.

Below: an artist's version of forging iron, a "firelight" painting by Joseph Wright. The great advance in mid-century was cheap steel.

Henry Bessemer discovered that steel could be produced cheaply by applying a hot blast to molten pig-iron in a "converter". Carbon was added after impurities had been expelled.

Engineers and Architects

Britain's greatest triumphs in the 19th century were, perhaps, in the field of engineering. Engineers were the heroes of the age, from railway builders, like Brunel and the Stephensons, to innovators like Bessemer, Whitworth, "Steam-hammer" Nasmyth and Sidney Gilchrist Thomas.

Men such as these gave Britain supremacy in industrial production; they built an intricate railway network at home and constructed railways in Europe, South America and across India. They also made ship-building a major industry in Glasgow, Belfast, Birkenhead and on Tyneside. British marine engineers played a leading part in the development of new ships, as iron and steel hulls replaced the wooden ships and steam took over from sail. They introduced screws to replace paddle-wheels, compound engines, triple and quadruple expansion engines and these were followed by Parsons' steam turbine.

This inventive energy did not extend to architecture. The Victorians failed to create a style in keeping with their age of machines, but turned instead to imitations of the past, from Classical styles to Gothic.

"The perfect Gothic home", an illustration from an architectural magazine, showing a supposed 13th century domestic interior.

The craze for imitation Gothic styles started as a whim but became almost the rule for the design of houses, churches, town-halls, railway stations and pubs. Pugin, who designed Birmingham Cathedral and parts of the Houses of Parliament, and Gilbert Scott were the leading exponents of this imitative style.

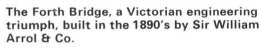

The Forth Bridge, a Victorian engineering triumph, built in the 1890's by Sir William Arrol & Co.

Left: Isambard Kingdom Brunel.

The Brunels

Isambard Kingdom Brunel (1806–59) and his father, Marc I. Brunel, were outstanding practical engineers. They worked together on the Thames Tunnel and on various public works before the son, Isambard, designed Clifton suspension bridge at Bristol.

He also designed three famous ships, the *Great Western*, the first steamship built for the Atlantic crossing, the *Great Britain*, the first large vessel with a screw-propeller, and the gigantic, ill-fated *Great Eastern*. Appointed engineer to the Great Western Railway in 1833, he constructed all its tunnels, bridges and viaducts.

Above left: Classical proportions of an American planter's home, the Linden Plantation, Mississippi. Americans were less obsessed with the Gothic craze than the British.

Above right: the Red House, Bexleyheath, designed by Philip Webb for William Morris.

Above: the Crystal Palace, Joseph Paxton's building of iron and glass.

Below: Guaranty Building, Buffalo, 1894, a skyscraper designed by Louis H. Sullivan, an American who pioneered steel buildings.

Domestic Gothic: villa complete with gable, capped turret, ornamental stonework and Tudor-style chimneys.

The Arts and Crafts Movement

The Arts and Crafts Movement came into existence in reaction to Victorian ugliness and bad taste. Though English in origin, it had a world-wide influence.

The movement had its beginnings in the Gothic revival, and came to centre around William Morris. He was a most remarkable man who started his career in an architect's office but soon turned to production of beautiful furniture, fabrics, glass and wallpapers. In 1861 he founded his own firm with his friends; Rossetti, Burne-Jones and Madox Brown, the painters, Philip Webb, an architect, Peter Marshall and Charles Faulkner.

Carefully choosing their workmen, they began making furniture and fabrics which set new standards of craftsmanship and simple design. Though derided in some quarters, the movement spread. Local organizations of craftsmen sprang up in various places under the leadership of gifted designer-craftsmen. New schools of art also had powerful influence on taste. A movement which started by looking back at the medieval past became one which looked forward to a new society in which art and good design should be part of everyone's life.

Photograph showing the Majolica Fountain in the Eastern Dome of the International Exhibition, 1862.

This pottery fountain is a supreme example of the confusion of styles and fussy ornamentation that characterized Victorian taste. Other examples include the Albert Memorial, the Law Courts in London and countless railway stations and villas with turrets and battlements.

The Furniture Court at the Great Exhibition of 1851, when British furniture reached an all-time low in grotesque design. This was what Morris and his friends were rebelling against. Commercial firms catered for a prosperous class that was easily fooled into thinking that showy ornament was the hall-mark of quality. Their pride was hurt when all the major awards at the Exhibition went to foreign designers.

Stained glass made by Morris's firm.

Attic bedroom designed by Ford Madox Brown, 1861. This cool, simple style did not commend itself to those who liked comfortable cosiness.

William Morris, a portrait by the famous Victorian artist, G. F. Watts.

Contrast to mid-Victorian taste: a Morris and Co. room with Morris Pomegranate wallpaper (1864), rush-seated chairs and furniture designed by Philip Webb. Burne-Jones painted the wardrobe on the left and designed the framed tiles on the wall. Morris himself painted the chest on the right. Webb designed the copper candles.

Morris, who hated cluttered rooms and fussy decoration, said, "Have nothing in your houses that you do not know to be useful or believe to be beautiful".

Agriculture

British farming did well during the Napoleonic Wars but the prosperity was followed by twenty years of depression. A revival occurred before the middle of the century and then came twenty booming years, a Golden Age, lasting from about 1850 to 1870. After 1875, a depression set in, from which British farming never fully recovered until World War Two.

Nevertheless, farming remained the largest single industry in the country. It employed nearly two million workers in 1851 and, although this figure had fallen to one and a half million by 1871, food production and acreage under cultivation increased. This was due to new techniques, fertilizers and better drainage, along with some mechanization. Progressive farmers spread their land with crushed bones, guano, newly-invented super-phosphates and nitrates from Chile or local gas works. They fed their livestock with oil-cake, maize and cheap imported grain. These techniques produced high grain yields, high meat production and high profits. A series of wet seasons in the late 1870's, and the flooding in of cheap American wheat and frozen meat, brought this prosperity crashing into ruins.

Old Smithfield Market in 1855. A new market was opened there in 1868.

Consumption of meat rose steadily during the second half of the century due to a general rise in wages. Farmers producing beef did well in Britain until the advent of frozen meat from abroad in the 1880's.

The first ship to bring frozen meat from New Zealand in 1882.

Below: shipping live cattle to England from America in 1877.

British Farming

As we have seen (page 4), the Corn Laws were introduced to protect farmers from the import of cheap foreign corn. They kept up the price of bread and this hurt the poor, but the effects of the Corn Laws may have been exaggerated. When they were repealed in 1846, the price of corn remained where it had been during the previous five years and it stayed steady for the next twenty years.

The price of wheat fell in the 1880's and 1890's from about 50s. a quarter to below 23s., bringing about the ruin of British agriculture. The crisis for British farming was due to two inventions; the railway and the steamship.

Railways had opened up the American prairies where farmers, using reaping machines and Mc-Cormick combine-harvesters, extracted enormous crops from virgin soil. The grain was carried by rail to the seaports to be shipped to Britain in the new steamships and sold at prices which brought ruin to the British farmer.

Switching to meat might have saved him but the 1880's saw the introduction of refrigeration and the arrival in British markets of cargoes of frozen meat from abroad.

Speenhamland

The Speenhamland system, begun in 1795, lasted until 1867. It was a scheme, originally intended to help the needy, whereby local authorities would pay out small allowances in times of hardship. In fact, farmers used it as an excuse to pay their labourers low wages.

The labourer's lot had worsened, for he had lost his strips of land and common rights. Chances of earnings from cottage spinning and weaving had vanished as the factory system developed. When farming prosperity collapsed, his best hope was to emigrate.

Left: a hungry labourer.

Right: Gentlemen of the Royal Society inspect the latest farm machinery.

A straw-burning steam-plough of 1874. Only the big landowners could afford these monsters. Most farmers still ploughed with horses.

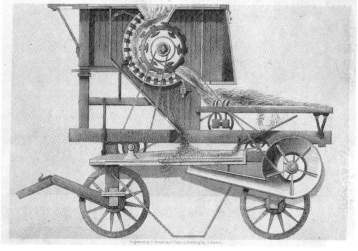

Garrat's improved threshing-machine (more popular than reaping-machines.) Labour was plentiful in Britain so farms were less mechanized than in America.

A double-cylinder steam-plough. A wire hawser drew the plough across the field, but the steam-plough was an expensive fad and never part of the ordinary working farmer's equipment.

The agricultural stand in the Great Exhibition, 1851. All kinds of new machines were on show—threshing-machines, turnip-slicers, rotary-diggers and improved implements such as ploughs and harrows.

Darwin's Voyage

In December 1831, a British naval survey vessel, H.M.S. *Beagle*, set off on a world voyage. The official naturalist on board was a young man named Charles Darwin, an amateur botanist who intended entering the Church. Throughout the five-year voyage, he made expeditions ashore to study animals, birds, insects, plants and rock formations.

At this time, almost everyone believed that God had created the world in six days and that man and all the creatures of the earth had sprung suddenly into existence. During the *Beagle's* voyage, Darwin compiled masses of evidence to refute this view. His observations taught him that the world had evolved over millions of years. Each species had developed and adapted itself to the struggle for existence—or had died out.

After his return to England, Darwin published his theory in a book called *On the Origin of Species*. It caused a sensation and aroused furious opposition from people who thought, wrongly, that Darwin claimed that man was descended from an ape. Despite the indignation, Darwin's book brought about an intellectual revolution. The world was never the same again.

Charles Darwin.

Thomas Huxley, eminent biologist, who accepted Darwin's theory and defended him against attacks.

Voyage Around the World

The picture above shows H.M.S. *Beagle* in Sidney Harbour. Her commander was Lieutenant Fitzroy, a man who believed completely in the literal truth of the Bible and argued angrily with Darwin. Fitzroy spent some three years surveying South American coastal waters and then took his ship to the Galapagos Islands, Tahiti, New Zealand, Australia and South Africa.

Darwin was able to spend long periods ashore, making cross-country journeys, climbing mountains and collecting thousands of specimens. Many of these he preserved and sent back to England.

He found bones of extinct monsters, plants and creatures unknown to European naturalists. In the Andes, he came across seashells at 12,000 feet which indicated vast upheavals of the earth's surface.

As he recorded his findings in his journal, he developed his theories about evolution which were to shake the Victorian world. His *Journal of the Voyage of the Beagle* was published in 1839 but he spent another twenty years of study before he felt ready to express his brilliant theory in *On the Origin of the Species* which was published in 1859.

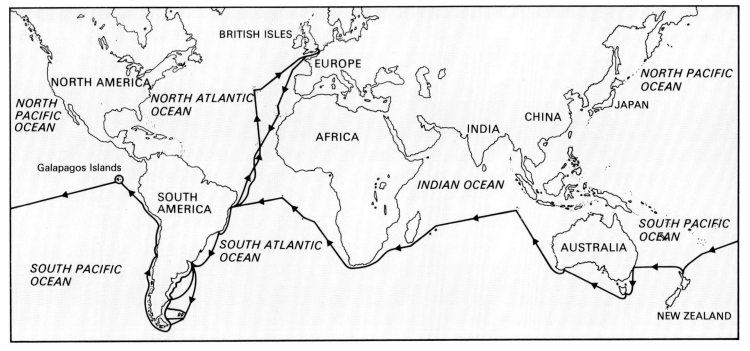

The voyage of the *Beagle*. Only 90 feet long, she was at sea for five years without a mishap.

Sailor overturns a giant tortoise on the Galapagos Islands where Darwin found many unique forms of life.

Darwin's tanager, a South American bird identified by Darwin and named after him. He became expert at preserving his specimens.

Land iguana, Galapagos Islands, where Darwin realized that life had evolved from primitive beginnings.

Cactus-eating finches, whose beaks varied according to their food.

Artists

In the 18th century, most artists had been commissioned by rich patrons for private collections. Now, with new public galleries opening, and new ways of printing and engraving reproductions, art reached a wider public.

Official art encouraged good draughtsmanship, and little attention was paid to light and colour. Pictures were designed to "tell a story" in ways that many now consider dull, or sentimental. Sir Edwin Landseer was a famous artist of this type.

Yet the century also produced artists of great genius. Constable combined love of nature with a fine sense of colour and harmony, while Turner created masterful studies of mist, cloud and sea. Encouraged by the critic, John Ruskin, the Pre-Raphaelites tried to recapture the spirit of medieval romanticism in contemporary as well as historical scenes.

Later, three great artists emerged in America; Winslow Homer and Albert Ryder, both fascinated by the sea, and Thomas Eakins, mostly a portrait painter. In London, Steer, Sickert and Whistler developed daring new techniques under the influence of the French Impressionists.

Rain, Steam and Speed by J. M. Turner, a painter obsessed by light and shade.

Derby Day by William Frith (1818–1909), one of a series of pictures of everyday English life (see also *The Railway Station*, page 9). He shows keen humorous observation and skill in grouping his figures.

Left: *La Belle Iseult* by William Morris, one of the Pre-Raphaelite group which included Rossetti; Millais, Holman Hunt, Burne-Jones and Ford Madox Brown. This painting shows their fascination with the medieval period. Others, like Brown's *Work* on page 2, point out moral themes in daily life.

Below: *La Dame aux Camelias* by Aubrey Beardsley, 1894. His work, now enjoying a revival, has a "decadent" flavour—he worked in black and white and his drawings conjure up a sense of evil.

Politics and Reform

In 1830, the Whigs came to power, pledged to do away with the Tory-supported system whereby tiny "rotten boroughs" with only a few voters returned members to Parliament, while great towns like Birmingham and Manchester had no member at all. But the House of Commons rejected the Reform Bill, whereupon the Whig Prime Minister, Earl Grey, dissolved Parliament. There followed the most excited General Election in history. When the new Commons passed the Bill, the Lords threw it out. Grey resigned and Wellington became Prime Minister. Public indignation was so fierce that Wellington bowed out, Grey came back and the Bill was passed in 1832.

The Bill only extended the vote to the middle-classes. The workers who had rioted for the Reform Bill still had no vote and there arose agitation for the "People's Charter". Its supporters demanded a vote for every householder, secret ballots, equal electoral districts, abolition of property qualification for M.P.'s, payment of M.P.'s and annual parliaments. In 1848, a monster petition was drawn up, but it proved to be a ludicrous failure and Chartism was laughed out of existence. However, in the long run, the Chartists did not fail. Disraeli and Gladstone put through most of their demands.

Below: Chartist petition, organized by Feargus O'Connor, on its way to Westminster in April 1848.

Benjamin Disraeli, who created the modern Conservative Party. He championed the workers, carrying through the Second Reform Act and aiding the trade unions. Abroad, he secured the Suez Canal for Britain and made Victoria Empress of India. The Queen, who loathed his rival, Gladstone, adored her charming "Dizzy".

William Ewart Gladstone, Liberal Prime Minister four times, a sombre giant who was a great Free Trader and a reformer who cared passionately for social justice. He sympathized with oppressed nations and adopted a high moral tone in foreign affairs. But he never succeeded in giving Home Rule to Ireland.

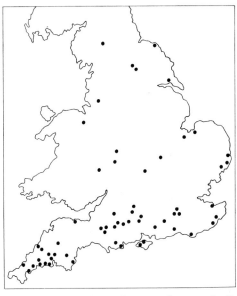

Distribution of the "rotten boroughs" before the 1832 Reform Act, when powerful landlords could control the voting in small towns. The industrial North and the Midlands were poorly represented, whereas Cornwall had 44 members. The Reform Act abolished 143 seats and redistributed them to the counties and large towns.

Trade Unions and Socialism

Pitt's Combination Acts of 1799 and 1800 were repealed in 1825. Trade unions were now legal, but they still had to face the implacable hostility of employers. In 1834, six farm labourers, the "Tolpuddle Martyrs", were transported for taking "illegal oaths" when forming a union.

To counter the power of authority, Robert Owen founded a giant union for all workers, but his Grand National Consolidated Union of 1833 failed through lack of finance and unity. After this fiasco, unions tended to become friendly societies giving help to members who were sick or unemployed. Early unions like the Amalgamated Society of Engineers (1851) adopted a moderate attitude which lulled employers' fears and won various concessions like the right to picket peacefully and legal protection of union funds.

From the 1870's, as Britain's prosperity began to fade, union leaders took up a more aggressive stance. Men like John Burns, Tom Mann and Keir Hardie shared Karl Marx's opposition to capitalism. But the mass of workers preferred the more genteel approach of the Fabian Society and the policy adopted was to improve working-class conditions through political means. In 1893, Hardie founded the Independent Labour Party to represent the workers in Parliament.

Opposite page: certificate of membership of the Gas Workers and General Labourers Union.

The Dockers' Strike

London dockers (notice the bowler hats!) vote in favour of a strike at West India Dock in 1889.

Members of earlier trade unions were mostly skilled workers and it was not until 1886 that the first of the great unions for unskilled workers was formed. This was the Dockers' Union, organized by Ben Tillett. Three years later, he led the dockers in their strike for a wage of sixpence (2½p) an hour. He was helped by John Burns and Tom Mann, leaders of the Amalgamated Society of Engineers. Their co-operation marked a new phase in trade union history.

The dockers could also count on public support, for it was well-known that they were wretchedly paid for work that was hard and intermittent. Hence, after a month's struggle, the employers conceded the main demand of sixpence an hour.

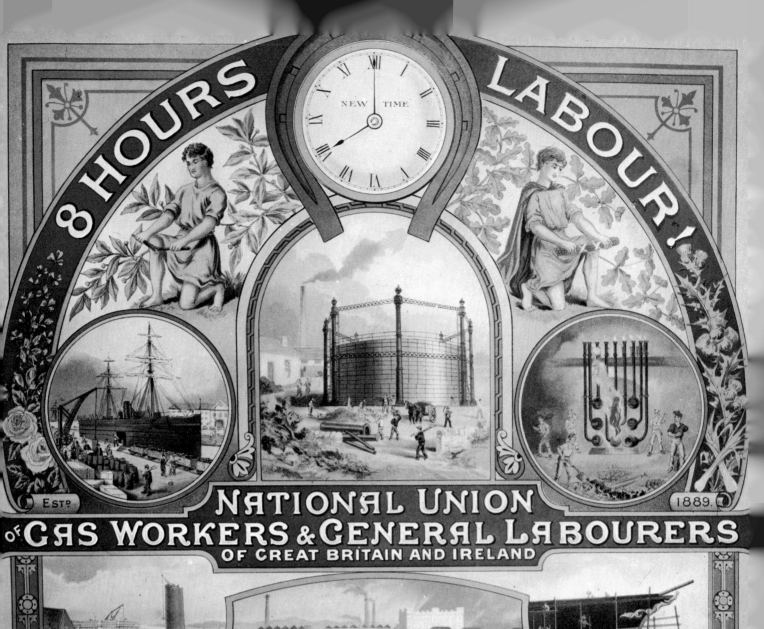

8 HOURS **LABOUR!**

NEW TIME

ESTD

NATIONAL UNION
OF GAS WORKERS & GENERAL LABOURERS
OF GREAT BRITAIN AND IRELAND

1889.

This is to Certify that

was admitted a Member of the above
Union on the   th day of   13

Secretary

Poverty and Social Reform

Novelists like Dickens and Disraeli, social observers like Charles Booth and Mayhew, together with numerous official reports, give us a horrifying picture of the conditions of the poor in Victorian times. Long hours, low wages, child labour, appalling slums and an almost total neglect of public health produced an urban working-class that was mostly stunted, ill-nourished, ignorant and degraded. Employers believed that better wages and conditions would upset the balance of society and bring industry to ruins.

However, the agitation of reformers like Shaftesbury and Dickens, and the public horror at outbreaks of cholera and typhoid led to some improvement. The Public Health Act of 1875 obliged towns to appoint medical officers of health; sewage and water systems were installed; the Artisans Dwellings Act encouraged councils to demolish slums and build working-class houses. Besides official action, much was done by private individuals like Octavia Hill who tackled slum housing, Dr Barnardo who founded homes for destitute children and William Booth who created the Salvation Army.

The Earl of Shaftesbury (1801–85) who worked ceaselessly for the poor, campaigning in Parliament and outside for better treatment of workers, paupers, children and prisoners. He was a founder of the Ragged Schools and a champion of the chimney-sweeps.

Left: Victorian provision for the homeless—Field Lane refuge, 1859. Some help for the destitute was provided by Poor Law authorities. Inadequate parish workhouses took in a few of the sick and aged, as well as pauper mothers and children.

Above: a slum in the East End of London, a print by Gustave Doré.
In thirty years, the population of London more than doubled. Housing was so scarce that three or four families commonly lived in a single room or cellar.

A girl at work in a South Carolina cotton-mill. Child labour was not peculiar to Britain but was found in all industrial countries. The factory system needed people willing to work for low wages. It was difficult to prevent children from working: poor parents needed the money and employers needed their labour. Both supported the system.

Visit of Prince Albert to the Soup Kitchen, Leicester Square, London. Albert and many rich people made sincere efforts to relieve the misery of the poor but the problems were too great for private charity. Government action was needed but, in the age of self-help, this was looked upon as interference with personal liberty and a threat to the economic system.

Dickens

In novels like *Bleak House, Nicholas Nickleby, Oliver Twist, David Copperfield* and *Hard Times*, Dickens brought an immense public to feel some of his own indignation against workhouses, debtors' prisons, bad schools and heartless officials. He looked at life through the eyes of the urban poor and tried to make the middle-classes see that cruelty and greed were social crimes. Yet even Dickens could not bring himself to describe the vice, filth and moral degradation that existed in Victorian London.

Charles Dickens (1812–70) the great novelist and reformer who never forgot the wretchedness of his own boyhood.

Right: a scene from *Nicholas Nickleby* Mrs Squeers dishes out medicine to the ill-fed, brutally treated inmates of Dotheboys Hall, a "farming" school in Yorkshire to which unwanted boys were sent by cruel guardians.

A street scene in a Newcastle slum in about 1880. Towns in the North of England had increased in size as rapidly as London, and the slums of Manchester, Liverpool and Glasgow were notorious. In Liverpool, one family in five lived in a cellar.

Health

By the end of the century, everyone except the very poor could expect a longer, healthier life. In Britain, it took two cholera epidemics before people realized the need for public health authorities—the feeling had been that they would "interfere" in people's private affairs. With London in the lead, thanks to John Simon, its first Medical Officer of Health, towns began to have clean water and efficient sewage systems. Steps were taken to supervise markets and slaughterhouses, to improve the quality of food and drink. Milk, for example, could now come into towns from farms, by railway, instead of being provided by cows kept in cellars and back-yards.

In medicine, Louis Pasteur proved what others had suspected—that disease was caused by tiny organisms known as "bacteria". From Pasteur came the practice of sterilizing, or "pasteurizing" milk. Lister applied this principle to surgery from 1865, so that, with the use of antiseptics, operations became less dangerous. They were already less agonizing, for James Simpson had introduced chloroform in 1847.

More than 170 specialist hospitals were opened in Britain, to deal with sick women and children, and such diseases as fever, paralysis and tuberculosis. Hospital equipment, from bandages, sheets and beds to food and drink, was greatly improved, but the biggest advance came with the arrival of a new type of nurse. From 1860, nurses were given training, uniform, and better working conditions.

Teeming slums created by the Industrial Revolution. In such conditions, disease and high death-rate were inevitable.

Britain's population and emigration statistics, 1821–1901. The white lines show that in England and Wales the population increased from about 12 million to 33 million. Scotland's increase was much less dramatic, while the population of Ireland fell, owing to potato famines and high emigration.
Emigration figures for the whole of Britain are measured in thousands by the black line on the graph.

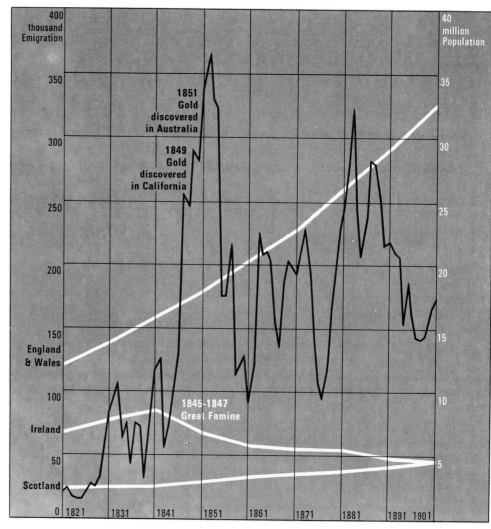

A Federal field hospital at Antietam, during the American Civil War. American army doctors were better prepared than the British had been during the Crimean War. Prior to the Civil War, they were issued with a comprehensive hand-book dealing with military hygiene, battle surgery, anaesthetics and vaccination.

Elizabeth Garrett Anderson (1836–1917), the first woman in Britain to qualify as a doctor; after great opposition, she obtained the Society of Apothecaries' diploma in 1865. Her example led to the founding of the London School of Medicine for Women in 1874. Her daughter Louisa was to take part in the movement for women's suffrage.

Florence Nightingale in a military hospital which is clean and spacious after her improvements.

Below: Florence Nightingale seated with a group of "new" nurses at St Thomas's, 1886.

Florence Nightingale

During the Crimean War, reports in *The Times* caused an outcry about conditions in the military hospitals, so Florence Nightingale was sent to Scutari with a party of nurses. She took control from the army authorities and introduced drastic reforms in cleanliness, equipment and food.

Back in England as a heroine, she devoted her life (from an invalid couch) to creating a nursing profession. She supervised all arrangements for the Nightingale School of Nursing, opened in 1860 at St Thomas's Hospital. Mrs Wardroper became its efficient superintendent for 27 years.

Police and the Criminal

For centuries, preservation of law and order in Britain depended upon local magistrates who called on parish constables and, in times of riot, on the army. In 1825, London had no more than about 300 constables to protect a city of over a million inhabitants. Respectable persons lived in dread of the London mob which could terrorize the capital for days on end, as it had done during the Gordon Riots.

The death penalty was imposed for more and more offences but, without an efficient police force, criminals generally went unpunished. As Home Secretary, Peel believed that the certainty of some kind of punishment was a better deterrent than the possibility of the death penalty. Influenced by Samuel Romilly's earlier pleadings, he swept away a mass of outdated laws and abolished capital punishment for over a hundred offences. In founding the Metropolitan Police, he had to face fierce opposition from an unruly public and from responsible persons who believed that a police force would be an instrument of tyranny. His civilian force proved to be nothing of the kind and London's example was copied all over the country.

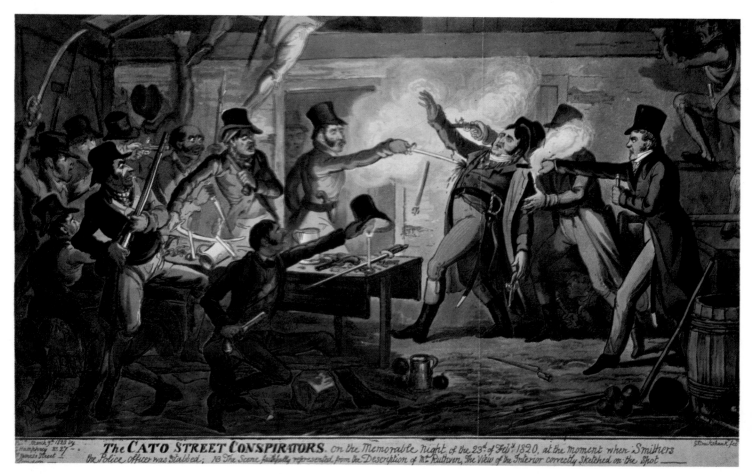

The CATO STREET CONSPIRATORS. on the Memorable night of the 23d. of Feby 1820. at the moment when Smithers the Police Officer was Stabbed; NB The Scene faithfully represented from the Description of Mr. Ruthven, The View of the Interior correctly Sketched on the Spot

Murder of a police officer who surprised the Cato Street conspirators. A police agent had probably been introduced into the gang to learn their plans.

The Cato Street Conspiracy

The Cato Street conspiracy centred about Arthur Thistlewood, a republican agitator who plotted revolution for several years and was known to the authorities as a dangerous man.

One night in February 1820, he and his friends were arrested in a loft in Cato Street, near the Edgware Road, as they were arming themselves to murder the Cabinet at dinner. An officer was stabbed during the arrest, but the conspirators were taken. Five of the conspirators were publicly hanged and five transported for life.

The Cato Street incident strengthened the hand of those who advocated a regular police force.

"Peelers"

The "Peelers" were highly unpopular at first because they had to be paid for out of the rates. All kinds of people from criminals to M.P.'s thought that they would obstruct the Englishman's right to do as he liked.

Peel had them looking like civilians rather than soldiers; they wore top hats, blue tailcoats

Cartoon ridiculing Peel's new police, known as "Peelers" and "Bluebottles".

and brown overcoats in winter. They carried no weapons except a truncheon and a rattle to summon help. The force, whose headquarters was in Scotland Yard, was divided into seventeen divisions, each under a superintendent.

Sir Robert Peel who founded the Metropolitan Police in 1829. He said, "Liberty does not consist in having your house robbed by organized gangs of thieves."

Fagin in the death cell, an illustration from Dickens' *Oliver Twist*. Dickens had first-hand knowledge of prisons, for his father was an inmate of the Marshalsea, a debtor's prison, where young Charles came to visit him on Sundays.

London had about 18 prisons at this time, most of them overcrowded, insanitary and run by corrupt, brutal overseers. The prison population consisted of murderers, thieves and minor offenders all herded together without occupation or training. Debtors could not obtain their liberty until their creditors had been paid.

Elizabeth Fry in Newgate prison where she found 300 women crowded into four filthy rooms. Many were famished and half-naked. They had sold their clothes to obtain food, since prisoners had to pay for meals. Mrs Fry formed an association to help women prisoners, found them work and taught their children. Other prison reformers included John Howard and Samuel Romilly.

A Child's Life

The child from a well-to-do Victorian home was brought up in nursery and schoolroom by nannie, governess and tutor who, if they lacked professional training, understood the value of discipline and hard work. Life may have been strict, but there were books and toys in plenty, besides holidays at the seaside and visits to the theatre and circus. Children from poor homes, less robust and shorter in stature, were lucky to attend school until the age of nine or ten. Thereafter they went to work in factory, mine, shop or on the land. In big cities, hordes of ragged waifs roamed the streets and lived by picking and stealing.

Like decent wages and housing, universal education was opposed by many who thought it dangerous to encourage the poor to question their position in life. However, Board Schools were established in 1870. They provided only the bare bones of education at first, but the curriculum gradually expanded as more teachers were trained. New private schools were founded, including some for girls, while the old grammar schools began to rouse themselves. Educational opportunity continued to be better in Scotland than in England, where a poor boy's best hope of higher education lay in attending night-school or one of the new polytechnics.

"Good Morning", an illustration from a Victorian children's book. It shows the night nursery, a plainly furnished room where no heating was allowed, except during illness. The day nursery was cosier, with its fireplace and high fender, table for meals and lessons, and the toys—rocking-horse, doll's house, boxes of soldiers and clockwork train.

The nursery staff probably included nurse, under-nurse and nursery maid in a big family. Mama visited the nursery briefly, like some remote goddess.

Page from *Under the Window* (1878) by Kate Greenaway, one of the most popular illustrators of children's books. Colour printing, which became commercially profitable from the 1830's, made books much more attractive.

"Toybooks", illustrated by Walter Crane, Randolph Caldecott and Kate Greenaway are now sought after by collectors. *Peter Rabbit*, written and illustrated by Beatrix Potter in 1893, did not appear publicly until 1902.

Left: clockwork dancing figures made during the 1860's. Mechanical toys were popular, but the favourites were Noah's Arks, dolls with wax or china faces, tops, hoops, toy theatres and building-blocks.

Right: toy theatre of about 1850, set with a scene from *Sleeping Beauty*. Children bought printed sheets of characters, cut them out, stuck them on card and moved them on the stage on wire slides.

Education

Until the Education Act of 1870 introduced public elementary schools, most English children went to the National or British Schools provided by the Churches. These were grim places where huge classes were given the rudiments of education by a teacher aided by monitors.

Some children had only a year or two at a Dame School run by an old woman, or learnt to read at Sunday School. Others had no schooling at all until the Earl of Shaftesbury started what became known as "Ragged Schools" for orphans and waifs.

Private schools of various kinds catered for middle- and upper-class children whose education would have begun with Nurse.

Left: a lesson in dental hygiene in about **1898**.

A Ragged School.

Grammar School, Mill Hill.

Regent Street Polytechnic, London.

Novels and Newspapers

Whatever may be said about Victorian artistic taste, nothing can detract from the splendour of Victorian literature. Greater leisure, wider education and the absence of other forms of entertainment made this the great age of the novel.

Jane Austen and Sir Walter Scott, neither of them Victorians but both immensely popular throughout the century, had already created a taste for novels when Dickens appeared on the scene. *Pickwick Papers* (1837) made him famous overnight. There followed a stream of brilliant novels whose characters became like real people to millions of readers. Nor was he the only giant. Thackeray, Hardy, George Eliot, Meredith, Trollope and the Brontë sisters proved that great literature and great popularity could go hand-in-hand.

The press and the novel were closely linked, for writers like Dickens often published their work first in serial form in magazines. The stories had to be exciting, and, at the end of a chapter, the author would often try to keep his readers hanging in suspense so that they would buy the next issue of the magazine.

Above: Thomas Hardy, who saw life as cruel and purposeless. Below: Charlotte Brontë whose masterpiece was *Jane Eyre*.

Above: W. M. Thackeray. His work is often compared with Dickens', but he was cooler, more cynical and less fond of humanity. *Vanity Fair* is perhaps his greatest novel.
Below left: George Eliot whose masterly novels include *Adam Bede* and *The Mill on the Floss*.
Below right: Mark Twain, creator of Tom Sawyer and Huckleberry Finn.

Photography waggon, Crimean War, 1854. Few newspapers carried pictures until the middle of the century, when *The Illustrated London News* appeared with engravings of people and events in the news. Photographs and sketches made on the spot were copied by the engraver.

William Russell, *The Times'* war correspondent Crimea. His reports, relayed by telegraph, shock public by exposing inefficiency and suffering. T caused the government to resign.

COLLEGE OF BLACK ART.

PROFESSOR OF SPIRIT-RAISING IN THE DOCK.

MAGIC BREASTPLATES.

WOMEN DUPES GO MAD.

(From Our Own Correspondent.)

NEW YORK, Tuesday, June 12.

The prosecution of Dr. Theodore White

LONELY HOUSE MURDER.

HUNTING FOR A TRAMP.

MYSTERY OF A BROKEN HAMMER.

WOUNDED SISTER'S STORY

Contrast in news presentation by the *Daily Mail* (above) and the *New York Journal* (below). Both were launched in 1896, the *Mail* by Alfred Harmsworth, the *Journal* by William Hearst. Both aimed for big circulations but the *Journal* was far more sensational.

NEW YORK JOURNAL
AND ADVERTISER

MISS EVANGELINA CISNEROS RESCUED BY THE JOURNAL.

An American Newspaper Accomplishes at a Single Stroke What the Best Efforts of Diplomacy Failed Utterly to Bring About in Many Months.

MISS CISNEROS BEFORE AND AFTER FIFTEEN MONTHS' INCARCERATION.

Diagram showing that, within two years of their founding, the cheap dailies had attracted huge readerships *The Times* remained static.

Ireland and Home Rule

Throughout the 19th century, the Irish question, like some menacing cauldron, kept coming to the boil. The causes of unrest were poverty and a dire land shortage. Ireland had no industry and her people lived almost solely on potatoes. To grow them, they needed land and there was not enough land to go round. In desperation, men offered absurd rents for any vacant plot and presently found themselves evicted from their holdings for failing to meet the rent. Blame was laid on English landlords and the English government.

Disastrous potato famines added to the people's misery and their only relief seemed to lie in emigration or in violence. With high motives, Gladstone determined to solve the Irish question, but, despite his land reforms, the Irish refused to be pacified. Most Irishmen wanted to be rid of the English, and Michael Davitt's Land League came to exert more power than the Government itself. Gladstone came to see that Home Rule (self-government) was the only solution. Alas, owing to Protestant Ulster's opposition and Parnell's downfall, he failed to achieve his dearest wish.

Uproar in the House of Commons where the Irish Home Rulers, inspired by Michael Davitt (inset) obstruct parliamentary business.
Led by Parnell, the Irish members made incessant speeches to draw attention to their cause and to bring the Government to a standstill.

Charles Stuart Parnell, "uncrowned King of Ireland", who was, oddly enough, a Protestant landowner.
A proud, reserved man, possessed of a burning passion to free Ireland from English rule, he united the Irish Nationalists and won over Gladstone to Home Rule. When a love affair brought him into the divorce court, his career was ruined.

Gladstone

For 25 years, Gladstone set his heart upon bringing a just solution to Ireland's problems. To remedy two major grievances, he put through an Act to disestablish the Irish (Protestant) Church, while his Land Act of 1870 was meant to protect tenants from eviction and to give them compensation for any improvements they made.

But the Irish remained discontented. Obstruction of Parliament and the violent activities of the Land League eventually convinced Gladstone that Ireland must be allowed to rule itself. So, in 1886, he brought in his first Home Rule Bill to put home affairs in the hands of a Dublin parliament. Not even his fellow Liberals would allow the Ulster Protestants to come under the rule of Catholic Nationalists and the Bill was defeated.

In 1892, the old man was Prime Minister for the fourth time and he introduced another Home Rule Bill (1893), proposing that Ireland should have its own parliament, with representation at Westminster to help direct imperial affairs. The Lords threw it out, Gladstone retired and died a few years later. With him died the last hope of Irish self-government for a generation.

Gladstone in the pulpit: he was a strict church-goer.

Police and soldiers carrying out an eviction. The authorities had an impossible task in trying to be fair to both landlords and tenants.

Captain Boycott, whose name brought a new verb into the English language, was a farmer and land agent in County Mayo.

He had given a rent rebate in 1879 to tenants hit by the potato famine but in the following year they demanded bigger rebates. His farm labourers went on strike, two landlords were murdered and Boycott was left to get in his harvest alone.

Eventually, a force of Ulstermen arrived to help him but the position of one Englishman surrounded by hostile neighbours became so impossible that the Boycotts had to quit their farm (above).

Left: an evicted family outside their home. The door has been smashed by the eviction party. So great was the demand for land that landlords could extort impossibly high rents and, when tenants failed to pay, could evict them at short notice.

Convicts and Free Settlers

By the time transportation ended, 148,000 convicts had served time in Australia and played their part in transforming that harsh land into a prosperous colony. Two thirds of the convicts came from England and about one third from Ireland. Most were sentenced to seven years transportation but they could earn their "ticket of leave" after four or five years and work for wages. Many prospered and few returned home.

Most of the free settlers came from Irish bogs, Scottish highlands and English farms. They made the immense journey be-

Ships at anchor in Botany Bay in Australia. The first convict ship arrived there in 1787, but the spot proved too inhospitable for settlement.

Dancing between decks on an emigrant ship.

cause they could not earn enough at home to keep their families from want. A few settlers came out with ample means to set up as landed gentlemen, and, in the time of the gold-rushes, thousands more poured into both countries in the hope of making a quick fortune. From the 1840's, New Zealand's settlers also included several groups carefully chosen by church associations—Scots in Otago and English in Canterbury district, for instance. These immigrants set higher than usual standards of education and conduct.

Lachlan Macquarie, Governor of New South Wales. He angered the free settlers by treating convicts humanely.

The Voyage Out

Conditions aboard the convict ships were appalling, but even the free settlers had to put up with great hardship. It was probably just as well that most emigrants had no idea of the hazards of the voyage.

Many of the ships were old and rotten; all were overcrowded and usually ill-supplied with rations by dishonest contractors. Some vessels never arrived. Many were lost at sea or wrecked off the dangerous coast of Victoria or in the Bass Strait that separates Australia from Tasmania. In 1866, for example, the steamer *London* went down in the Bay of Biscay with 223 emigrants.

By the 1850's sailing packets averaged eighty days from Liverpool to Melbourne; then came the magnificent clippers, faster than steamships, which made the trip in sixty days.

Until the underwater telegraph was laid at the end of the century, the arrival of an emigrant ship was eagerly welcomed, for it brought letters and news from "home". News of a new arrival was wired ahead from Sydney by reporters who had scanned the newspapers at an earlier port of call.

Emigrants to Australia take a stroll on deck—for most of the voyage they were kept below.

Left: a prison ship or "hulk" with convicts going aboard in Portsmouth Harbour.

Owing to the shortage of prisons, convicts were sent to the hulks, anchored in various ports, to wait there until a fleet of transport ships was assembled to carry them to Australia.

Australia and New Zealand

Gold was discovered in Australia in 1851 and the fortune-seekers who poured in brought a new spirit which helped complete the break with the convict past. When the gold fever died down, many of the "diggers" turned to the land and came into conflict with the big sheep-farmers. The ex-miners wanted farms or small sheep runs. After a long contest, both types of farming held their own. Australia's wealth, at this time, lay not in gold but in wool, wheat and cattle. The country experienced ups and downs, periods of prosperity followed by speculation and bank failures, until 1879, when the advent of refrigerated ships meant that vast quantities of meat could be carried to Britain.

New Zealand's progress was hampered by the Maori Wars. These affected the North Island more than the South Island, where timber, flax, whale oil, wool and meat were the chief products. Gold was discovered in the 1860's and during the next decade, under Julius Vogel, New Zealand advanced rapidly. Climate, good pasture and refrigeration made her, by the 1880's, the world's leading producer of dairy foods.

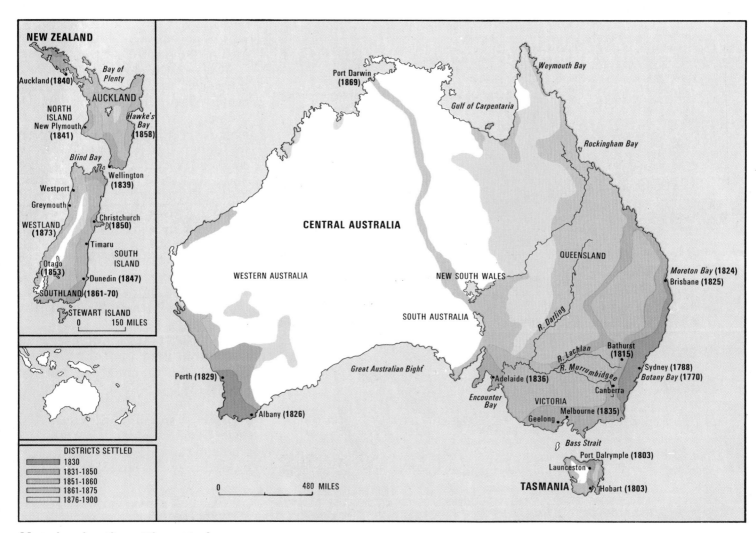

DISTRICTS SETTLED
- 1830
- 1831-1850
- 1851-1860
- 1861-1875
- 1876-1900

Map showing the settlement of Australia and New Zealand. Britain annexed New Zealand in 1840, and the founding of settlements went on steadily as immigrants arrived. In 1852, New Zealand was divided into six provinces, Auckland, New Plymouth, Wellington, Nebon, Canterbury and Otago.

Australia

The colony of Australia was confined to the coastal strip around Sydney until Blaxland crossed the Blue Mountains and discovered the Bathurst Plains in 1813.

In 1829–30, Sturt travelled down the Murrumbidgee to the sea. Meanwhile, Cunningham had pushed north to discover the Darling Downs behind Brisbane. Between 1860 and 1861 Burke and Wills crossed from Melbourne to the Gulf of Carpentaria.

Above: friendly overtures to Australian aborigines.

The benevolence did not last. The settlers advanced inland, driving the natives from their hunting-grounds into remote, arid regions.

Massacres took place; aborigines were shot like game and, in Tasmania, the original inhabitants were wiped out. In New Zealand, where the Maoris possessed a much higher culture, clashes occurred over land. The Maoris did not understand land-purchase and realized too late that they had lost their communal land for a few guns.

Right: Maori chief in about 1880.

V. R.

NOTICE!!

Recent events at the Mines at Ballaarat render it necessary for all true subjects of the Queen, and all strangers who have received hospitality and protection under Her flag, to assist in preserving

Social Order

AND

Maintaining the Supremacy of the Law.

The question now agitated by the disaffected is not whether an enactment can be amended or ought to be repealed, but whether the Law is, or is not, to be administered in the name of HER MAJESTY. Anarchy and confusion must ensue unless those who cling to the Institutions and the soil of their adopted Country step prominently forward.

His Excellency relies upon the loyalty and sound feeling of the Colonists.

All faithful subjects, and all strangers who have had equal rights extended to them, are therefore called upon to

ENROL THEMSELVES

and be prepared to assemble at such places as may be appointed by the Civic Authorities in Melbourne and Geelong, and by the Magistrates in the several Towns of the Colony.

CHAS. HOTHAM.

Appeal by the Governor of Victoria in 1854, after the Eureka Stockade tragedy when 150 discontented miners were overwhelmed by police and soldiers. Some 30 died.

Above: settlers in the Australian bush, outside the home that they have built from planks and have roofed with bark. Notice the verandah and home-made chair.

Below: Eagle Hawk Gully, Bendigo, one of the goldfields of the 1850's. Shack towns sprang up and were abandoned overnight on rumours of rich strikes elsewhere.

Canada

In the early part of the century, Canada consisted of Upper Canada (Ontario), Lower Canada (Quebec) and the Maritime Provinces. Grievances arose because the elected assemblies felt that English governors and their appointed councils ignored the colonists' interests and made grants of land to "outsiders" and to a Church which few of the settlers supported. Lord Durham was sent out to investigate the troubles which had caused two minor rebellions and, in his Report of 1839, he recommended that the provinces be joined under a responsible parliament. In short, he proposed that Canada should practically govern itself.

Union of the provinces, however, was not a success, for ill-feeling between French Canadians and British settlers had by no means died out. What was to be the next step? Absorption into the rich and powerful United States or the formation of a different kind of unity? The American Civil War convinced Canadians that the best step would be to found a confederation of all the provinces. This was achieved by the British North American Act of 1867.

Troops bivouac in the snow during the 1837–38 rebellions, when French Canadian extremists took up arms.

In Lower Canada, the French Canadians were determined to preserve their language and religion. They felt that the Governor and his appointed council thwarted the views they expressed in the assembly. In 1837, Louis Papineau led an uprising, but most of the French held back. Some street-fighting and village skirmishes took place before Papineau fled to the United States and the rebellion flickered out.

Canada and the Civil War

Canadian attitudes to the American Civil War were mixed. On the one hand, they were strongly against slavery and thousands of Canadians fought on the Federal side. On the other hand, they feared that a victorious northern army might annexe Canada. Relations became strained during the war, especially when southerners entered Canada and made raids across the border.

These incidents served to intensify the feeling that Canada's independence must be safeguarded and, in 1867, within two years of the war's end, Canadians had united their provinces into a confederation.

Left: Canadian stamp issued in 1917 to commemorate the fiftieth anniversary of the Confederation.

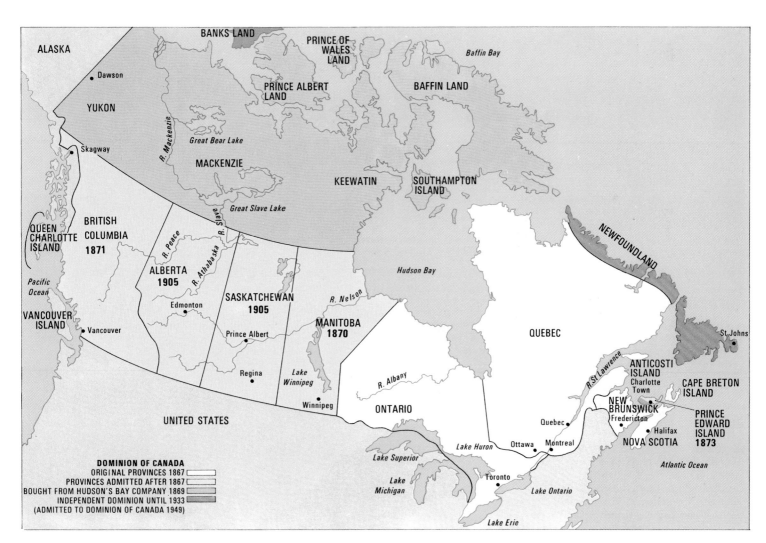

In 1867, the new Dominion began life in anything but a confident mood. Newfoundland declined to join and Prince Edward Island hung back.

Fortunately, in John A. Macdonald, the first prime minister, Canada found a man capable of surmounting troubles and suspicion. A new province, Manitoba, joined the Confederation in 1870 and British Columbia came in on the promise that a transcontinental railway would be built.

The Dominion of Canada set up in 1867 and the provinces admitted later. The vast northern areas were bought from the Hudson's Bay Company for £300,000 in 1869.

51

The British in India

The history of the British rule of India during the 19th century falls into two parts—before the Mutiny and after. Prior to 1857, the East India Company steadily extended its authority over vast areas. The rule of law and western ideas were introduced by administrators, most of whom held the view that India would come to govern herself.

Then came the Mutiny, a brief and bloody episode that was suppressed with comparative ease. But it left bitter feelings. Its causes had lain largely in the very reforms which the British had introduced. Afterwards the rulers felt it best to leave Indian society alone and concentrate upon administration. Queen Victoria was acclaimed Empress of India in 1877 and the idea of Indians ruling themselves was pushed into the remote future. However, in bringing the country together under one administration and in spreading education, the British were sowing the seeds of Indian nationalism. In 1885, when the first Indian National Congress met, its attitude was moderate; by the end of the century, the tone had become markedly anti-British.

A Viceroy of India, with his wife and daughter after a tiger-shoot. The British ruling class enjoyed lavish hospitality from the Indian Princes who were almost embarrassingly loyal to the Crown.

Right: map showing that about one third of India was not ruled directly by the British.

From Lord Wellesley's time (1798–1805), it was the East India Company's policy to make treaties with Indian princes. The rulers recognized the Company (and, later, the Crown) as the main power. They supplied military assistance when required and co-operated in matters like roads and railways which affected India as a whole.

In return, the princes retained their personal rule and were protected from aggression and rebellion. Occasionally, the British would depose a Maharajah who ruled badly.

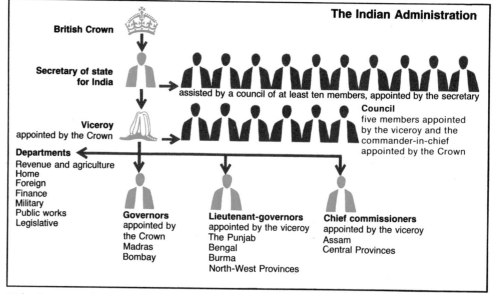

The diagram shows the complicated apparatus by which the British ruled India. In India itself, real power lay with the Viceroy, but he was limited by the instructions sent by the Secretary of State in England.

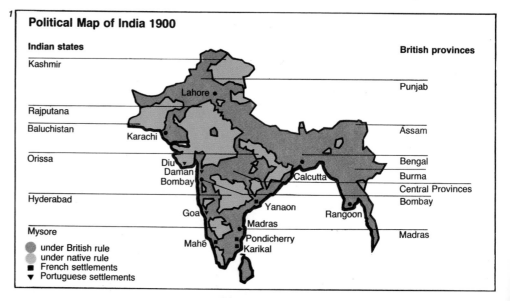

A New Prosperity

Besides peace and order, India gained in economic development. The second half of the century saw a boom in cotton-growing, the rise of the jute industry in Bengal and the establishment of tea-gardens in Assam.

New seaports and 25,000 miles of railway helped to bring Indian products to the world. Roads, telegraph and postal services improved communications and railways could move food into famine areas. Irrigation works brought millions of acres into production to feed India's ever-increasing population.

Left: an imposing symbol of the British _Raj_ (rule)—a railway terminus in Bombay.

The Sikh Wars

In 1845, Sikh leaders, alarmed by the British annexation of territories next to the Punjab, launched an attack on the foreigners. Battles at Mudki, Ferozeshah and Aliwal brought defeat to the Sikhs. They were forced, by the Treaty of Lahore, to cede some of their territory, including Kashmir.

John Lawrence took charge of part of the Punjab, but this was more than the proud Sikhs could stand and war broke out again in 1848. It ended with total defeat for the Sikhs and the annexation of the Punjab by the British.

Right: Battle of Mudki, 1848; Sir Hugh Gough fights a fierce battle with the Sikhs.

Sikh soldiers of the Punjab. The Sikhs did not join in the Mutiny. They respected John Lawrence and hated the Bengal army.

The Indian Mutiny, 1857

British rule was a threat to traditional life in India, and resented by many. Mutiny in the native army of Bengal was sparked off when cartridge grease made from the fat of cows and pigs was introduced, offending both Hindus and Moslems. The rebels seized Delhi and restored the Mogul Emperor. Massacres occurred at Cawnpore, while, at Lucknow, a tiny British garrison held out against huge odds.

Eventually, Lucknow was relieved and the Mutiny suppressed. But the Mutiny put an end to the East India Company.

War in the Crimea

The Crimean War rose out of the "Eastern Question"; Britain and France were nervous about Russian designs on Turkey and indeed, the Tsar had suggested carving up the Turkish Empire. This would have meant Russians in the Mediterranean and a threat to India.

The Turkish Sultan misgoverned most of the Balkans and, as Slavs and Orthodox Christians, the Balkan peoples looked to the Tsar for protection. In 1853, the Tsar found an excuse to occupy two Turkish provinces at the mouth of the Danube and then proceeded to destroy a Turkish fleet at Sinope. When Britain and France declared war in March 1854, the Emperor Napoleon III welcomed the chance of winning military glory and the British people, cocksure after years of peace, were in fighting mood.

The Crimean War proved to be one of the most muddled episodes in military history and it was concluded by a peace as futile as the conduct of the war. It was said that only two persons came out of the Crimea with credit—Florence Nightingale and the common soldier.

Balaclava harbour, an early war photograph.

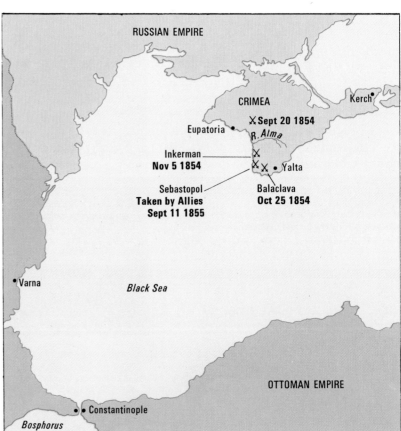

Map of the Crimean War. French and British troops landed at Eupatoria and defeated the Russians on the Alma. They might have then taken Sebastopol, but moved instead south-east to investigate the port, giving the enemy time to dig in.

In attempts to break the siege, the Russians attacked the British at Balaclava and fought a slogging infantry battle at Inkerman. By 1855, the Allies, better organized at last, captured Sebastopol and the war ended with the Treaty of Paris.

Left: British infantrymen at Gallipoli. Soldiers were ill-paid and ill-fed and the army went out without winter equipment or transport. More died from sickness than wounds and the medical services were chaotic until Florence Nightingale arrived. Nevertheless, armed with the new Minié rifle and bayonet, the troops fought with amazing courage.

Soldiers relaxing at the front. The photograph does not show the horror of the war described in William Russell's war despatches—soldiers in snow-filled trenches without warm clothing or soles to their boots. Men died for lack of stores which were stranded a few miles away for lack of wagons.

A paperweight depicting the Allied heads of state during the war. Queen Victoria is in the centre, Emperor Napoleon III on the right. Victoria and Albert visited Paris in 1855 to cement the new Franco-British alliance and found that they liked Napoleon and his dazzling Empress Eugenie.

The Charge of the Light Brigade

At Balaclava, the Russians captured some British guns and Lord Raglan ordered the cavalry to save them. Unfortunately, the order was not clear and was taken to mean a battery of Russian guns at the end of a well-guarded valley.

Led by Lord Cardigan, the Light Brigade charged down "the valley of death" and spiked the guns. Then the survivors rode back.

The Light Brigade reach the Russian guns. "Their's not to reason why, Their's but to do and die" wrote Tennyson. Out of 673, 113 were killed and 134 wounded.

Ships – from Sail to Steam

Among the spectators watching the trials of William Symington's novel steamboat, the *Charlotte Dundas*, in 1802, was Robert Fulton of Pennsylvania. He went home to build the *Clermont*, America's first paddlesteamer. In 1819, a New York ship, the *Savannah*, crossed the Atlantic with some help from her steam-driven paddles but it was not until 1827 that the Dutch *Curacao* made the first all-steam crossing.

After this, the story of steamships was one of progress in face of ridicule from the sailing men; steamers continued to carry sails for many years but wooden hulls were gradually replaced by iron. Paddle-wheels gave way to screws after Brunel's *Great Britain* steamed from Liverpool to New York in 1845. Rivalry between steam and sail went on throughout the century, with victory going to steam. More efficient engines were designed and the Suez Canal, suitable only for steamships, provided a shorter route to the East. Nevertheless, a glorious era for sail remained. On very long voyages, the magnificent clipper ships were able to hold their own with steam until well into the 20th century.

Poster advertising the 1,400 ton New York clipper *Hornet,* built in 1851, which made the fast time of 105 days to San Francisco via the Horn.

Right: a fanciful picture of a river "steam-train" at the time of the Indian Mutiny. Steamers played an essential role on Indian rivers, conveying troops and pulling barges called "flats", laden with jute and tea.

The *Red Jacket* in the ice of Cape Horn. She was a clipper that carried men to the California gold-fields.

ORIENT-PACIFIC LINE

Luxury liner of about 1900—the P.&O. S.S. *Ophir* at Port Said.

Shipping Lines

Regular sailings across the Atlantic were introduced to convey emigrants to Canada and the United States. From 1816, the Black Ball Line ran services between Liverpool and New York, taking about 33 days for the voyage out. Conditions aboard these packet ships were appalling but faster crossings were made from 1840 when Samuel Cunard founded the Cunard Steamship Company.

Emigrants could also travel cheaply on the iron steamers of the Inman Line. The most famous line to the East was the P. & O. (Peninsular and Oriental) which carried passengers, cargo and mail.

Towards the end of the century, sea-travel lost its terrors, as luxury liners competed for the new tourist trade on the Atlantic crossing.

A midnight race on the Mississippi by two steamboats. The Mississippi was America's great artery for trade and communication. It received water from 54 smaller rivers navigable by steam-boats and drained an area as big as Europe. In parts of the great river system, shallows and mudbanks would have impeded normal vessels, so American engineers designed flat-bottomed steamers that sat on the water and glided over it. Their machinery was placed on deck, instead of in the hold. The wheels were placed at the sides or in the stern, and smokestacks towered above.

America Takes Shape

By mid-century, "Manifest Destiny" had triumphed. This was a belief that it was the destiny of the Americans to spread across the whole continent. It led to the annexation of Texas and war with Mexico. Meanwhile, the frontier had been pushed westwards. Settlers poured through the Cumberland Gap or passed down the Erie Canal and along the rivers into the heart of the continent to found new states.

American democracy grew up in the valley of the Mississippi and the rise of democratic western states brought conflict with the East, which was suspicious of the growing political power of farmers and settlers. Down the Atlantic seaboard, there also developed antagonism between the North and the slave-owning South.

In seventy years, the West produced eleven out of eighteen Presidents. It also produced the traditional American. He was versatile and aggressively confident. Yet he was also impatient of discipline and all too often broke treaties with the Indians and drove them from their ancestral hunting-grounds. In the West, a man was valued, not for his birth, but for what he could do; equality of opportunity and the survival of the fittest were the lifeblood of this new nation.

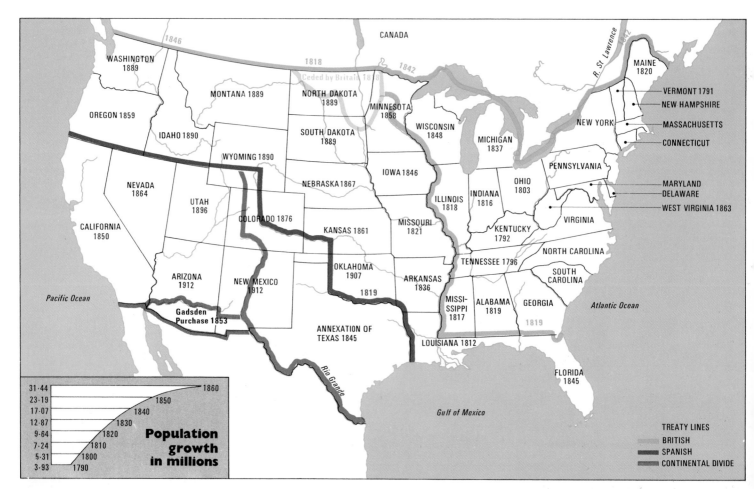

Growth of the Union: the states and the dates when they achieved full statehood. During the century, the population almost doubled itself every twenty years.

The Louisiana Purchase in 1803 added a million square miles to the Union (Louisiana then meant a vast area west of the Mississippi). The Indians were thrust back to make room for settlement. Texas broke away from Mexico and was then annexed in 1845, while the treaty that ended the Mexican War brought in California, Arizona and New Mexico. The Oregon Boundary dispute with Britain was settled in 1846 fixing the northern boundary west of the Great Lakes.

Crossing the Rockies, a lithograph by Currier and Ives. As early as 1804, Meriewether Lewis and William Clark made their epic journey across the Rockies, opening the way for other exploring ventures into the Far West.

Traders forged the Santa Fé Trail to the South-West, braving heat, drought and attacks by Comanche and Sioux Indians. By the 1840's, reports of rich farmland in Oregon and California persuaded thousands of pioneers to take the Oregon Trail across the Rockies.

They went in great covered wagons, "prairie schooners", strong enough to ford rivers, ascend rocky passes and withstand Indian arrows.

American troops enter Mexico City.

The United States annexed Texas, a former possession of Mexico, in 1845, and boundary disputes broke out.

After attempts to reach a settlement had failed, President Polk sent General Zachary Taylor into Texas to hold the Rio Grande river. The Mexicans attacked and were defeated in the stubborn battle of Buena Vista. Another American army under Winfield Scott landed at Vera Cruz and, by September 1847, Mexico City had fallen.

When peace was made, the United States received California and the huge area called New Mexico, which included the present states of Utah and Nevada.

The Monroe Doctrine

During the Napoleonic Wars, South America had broken away from its European masters. When peace came, Americans feared a return to colonial domination, possibly by Britain or France. In 1823, President Monroe baldly stated that interference in the New World would be regarded as an "unfriendly" act. The Monroe Doctrine remains a basis of American foreign policy.

James Monroe, fifth President of the United States of America, 1817–25.

President Jackson (1829–37)

Son of a Scottish-Irish immigrant, reared in poverty in western Carolina, Andrew Jackson became in turn a lawyer, frontier general and President of the United States.

In the 1812 War, "Old Hickory", as his soldiers called him, beat the British at New Orleans; later, he defeated the Creek Indians and invaded Florida. As President, Jackson was suspicious of rich bankers. One of his acts was to destroy the Bank of the United States. He had strong faith in the Federal government and, in 1830, refused to let South Carolina annul a Congress tariff law.

Gold, Cotton and Wheat

Two staple crops, cotton and wheat, played a major role in shaping America's growth and history. Her river transport system, canals, roads and railways were built mainly to carry these lucrative products to the world's markets.

Development of Eli Whitney's cotton gin revolutionized cotton production, which replaced tobacco as the basis of the South's economy. In the Cotton Kingdom, as it was called, small farms were bought up and combined into great plantations worked by slave labour. Cotton brought such profits that it was hardly worth growing anything else. The Cotton Kingdom's requirements in food and animals spurred the West into producing grain, meat and mules.

Wheat was always the great frontier crop. It required less labour than most other crops, grew in a tough concentrated form that made it easily stored or transported and it did particularly well on newly-broken soil. American reaping and threshing machines were the most advanced in the world and it was said that, thanks to McCormick's reaper, "the line of civilization moves westward thirty miles each year".

No sooner had the United States acquired California than gold was discovered on John Sutter's ranch. From 1849, the race was on, as thousands of fortune-hunters poured in to wash gold out of the gulches or to dig for it in the hills. The wealth that flowed out of California can only be compared with the riches that poured from South America to 16th-century Spain.

Below: a frontier town on one of the trails to the West. Hastily thrown up, these shack towns, with names like Poker Flat and Skunk Gulch, provided lodging and entertainment for the pioneers and gold prospectors.

Law meant nothing in the bars and gambling saloons and many a miner was fleeced of his gold dust.

Triumphant completion of America's first transcontinental railway. The Union Pacific built westward, the Central Pacific eastward; the lines met at Ogden, Utah, in 1869.

Gold washing in California, 1849, when 100,000 fortune-seekers managed to extract $10 million worth of gold from the streams and gulches.

Right: harvesting wheat on the prairies. On the far western plains, severe winters caused farmers to sow a new kind of spring wheat from the 1870's. Its hard grain yielded better flour than winter wheat.

Left: loading cotton on the Mississippi. In 1811, Robert Fulton built the first western steamboat, *New Orleans*. By 1830, nearly 200 steamboats were carrying cargoes of wheat and cotton to New Orleans. From there, shipments went to the eastern states and Europe. Hundreds of miles of canal were dug to help river transport. The Erie Canal, for example, linked the Hudson River and the Great Lakes.

Below: a cotton plantation on the Mississippi. The high profitability of cotton and its exhausting effect on the soil caused southerners to move on to the fertile lands of Alabama, Mississippi and Louisiana during the early part of the century.

As a crop, cotton needed large numbers of unskilled workers. The aristocratic plantation owners controlled a slave population that rose from one and a half million in 1820 to four million in 1860.

Slavery and the South

Cotton-growers needed slaves for the continuous unskilled work of cultivating, picking and packing the crop. Although many southerners disliked the system, they saw no other way of growing the cotton on which the South's economy depended. Most northerners wanted slavery totally abolished or at least confined to its old limits.

The clash occurred when the new territories of the West began to be settled. Were they to be slave states or free? Texas already had slavery; what about California and New Mexico which had not? What about the territories called Kansas and Nebraska?

Southerners felt that slavery should be a right in all the territories, but the North was mostly opposed to any extension of slavery. Some moderates felt that a line (the Missouri Compromise Line) could be extended, dividing the slave states from the free. Others supported "popular sovereignty", whereby the settlers in new territories should decide the question for themselves. But compromise proved impossible. As tension grew into hatred, the issue had to be decided by war.

The Olivier Plantation, Louisiana. Rich planters lived in lordly style; proud, hospitable and cultured, they feared that the bustling industrialized North would destroy southern interests. Slavery was essential to their way of life. At best, they were benevolent; at worst, heartless tyrants.

Slaves on a South Carolina plantation. Since 1808, importing slaves from Africa had been banned, but Virginia and Maryland specialized in rearing their own slaves for sale to the lower South.

A southern tobacco factory. Cotton demanded more slaves than tobacco.

Harriet Beecher Stowe who wrote *Uncle Tom's Cabin*.

Lincoln versus Douglas

A series of public debates took place in 1858, between Abraham Lincoln and Stephen Douglas. They were competing for senatorship of Illinois, and slavery was at the centre of their debates. Douglas claimed that the new territories had the right to decide on slavery for themselves; Lincoln claimed that Congress had the right to forbid it.

Douglas won Illinois, but the debates made Lincoln famous and he defeated Douglas in the elections for the Presidency in 1860. At once, South Carolina left the Union, and six other states followed to form a Southern Confederacy.

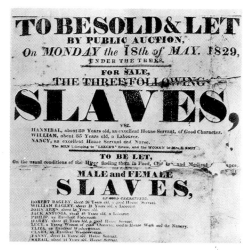

Poster advertising a slave auction in 1829 when a strong male slave would fetch about $1,000.

The Fugitive Slave Law

Uncle Tom's Cabin was a tremendous best-seller in the North and in Britain. It was written to focus indignation against the Fugitive Slave Law. The law meant that escaped slaves were denied jury trial, and Federal officers were ordered to capture them. Those assisting escapees were liable to fines or imprisonment. Northern abolitionists organized an "underground railway" to convey runaway slaves through the states to safety in Canada. Mobs sometimes attacked slave-catchers. The law worsened relations between North and South.

The American Civil War

When South Carolina left the Union in 1860, hostility between North and South had already led to bloodshed. In Kansas, pro-slavery and anti-slavery settlers had attacked one another and, in 1859, the fanatical abolitionist, John Brown, had raided Harper's Ferry in the hope of raising a slave rebellion. Yet there seemed little reason for the South to secede (leave the Union). Even if he had wished to do so, Lincoln could not abolish slavery and, in the case of a Negro called Dred Scott, the Supreme Court had ruled that it was unconstitutional to exclude slavery in the territories. So what did the southerners want? More and more, they had come to see the North growing stronger. It was now or never. If they became independent they could follow their own separate interests and acquire new land by annexing Cuba and Mexico.

The seceded states met to found a new nation and elected Jefferson Davis President of the Confederacy. Various government properties, mints, arsenals and forts, were seized but the commander of Fort Sumter, overlooking Charleston harbour, refused to co-operate. On 12 April 1861, the Confederate guns opened fire and, on the following day, Fort Sumter surrendered. The Civil War had begun. It was to last four years and cost over half a million lives.

Below: Abraham Lincoln, the President who steered the North to victory. His great aim was to preserve the Union. "The Union of these States is perpetual", he declared at his inauguration.

Typical of northern industrial superiority—the Colt weapons factory at Hartford, Connecticut. The North possessed far greater wealth, raw materials and industry. It had 30,000 miles of railways, besides lake, river and canal routes.

The South had almost no industry or skilled workers and possessed only two main railway lines.

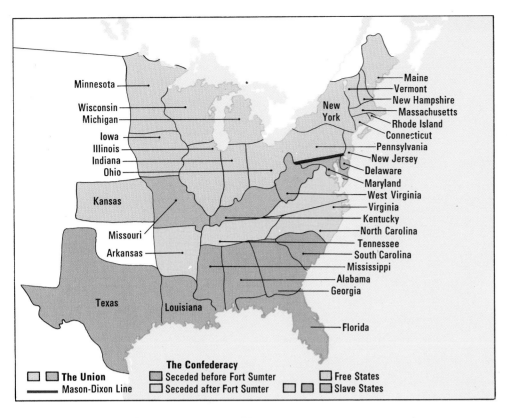

North and South

The six states that joined South Carolina in the Confederacy were Mississippi, Florida, Alabama, Georgia, Louisiana and Texas. After the attack on Fort Sumter, Virginia also seceded, though its western part remained loyal. Arkansas, Tennessee and North Carolina brought the Confederacy's numbers up to eleven. Four slave states, Missouri, Maryland, Kentucky and Delaware, stayed in the Union, giving the North a total population of 22 million against 9 million southerners, of whom one-third were Negroes.

Left: map showing the divided nation.

Above: the Confederacy issued its own money; as the war went on, this note became almost worthless.

Right: Union recruiting poster. Uniforms were provided by volunteers themselves or by their local towns.

The Outbreak of War

Hostilities began with the capture of Fort Sumter, whereupon Lincoln called for 75,000 militia to serve for 90 days. Volunteers poured into the training camps.

In July 1861, General McClellan drove a Confederate force back towards Richmond, the southern capital. With the main Union army, General McDowell then attacked the Confederate lines at Bull Run. But General "Stonewall" Jackson stood firm until reinforcements arrived and the raw Union volunteers fled in disorder back to Washington. After Bull Run, no-one believed the war would be a 90-day affair.

Left: the arrival of Major Anderson at Fort Sumter.

The Two Armies

If the Confederate forces had followed up their victory at Bull Run, they might have captured Washington and brought the war to an end. But the South was fighting a defensive war. Many believed that the Confederacy could win by simply holding on, so Jefferson Davis and General Joe Johnston concentrated their strength in front of Richmond without making any attacking move. Meanwhile, McClellan, an excessively cautious general, continued to train the Federal army; little happened in Virginia for eight months.

In the West, a hard-drinking Brigadier-General named Ulysses Grant captured the Confederate strongpoints of Fort Henry and Fort Donelson, but lost 13,000 men in the drawn battle of Shiloh. However, the Confederate losses were also heavy; General Albert Johnston was killed and Corinth had to be abandoned. While Halleck and Grant inched southwards, a joint army-navy operation under General Butler and Admiral Farragut captured New Orleans. Apart from the Confederate stronghold of Vicksburg, the whole of the Mississippi, from north to south, was now in Union hands.

McClellan, Union general.

Robert E. Lee, Confederate general.

The First Modern War?

In many ways, Napoleon and Wellington would have felt perfectly at home during the American Civil War.

The armies still consisted basically of cavalry, infantry and guns. The cavalry was used principally for reconnaissance and the infantry advanced as a rule in close columns. There was no significant change in the employment of artillery.

The strategic use of railways, however, the electric telegraph and the involvement of the civilian populations, were new. In the intensity of hatred, in the sheer number of troops and the appalling casualties, this was indeed a modern war.

Both sides began by calling for volunteers and then introduced conscription. By the end of the war, the North had enlisted more than two million men and had a million in the field, while, from a smaller population, the Confederate South had enlisted between 700,000 and 1,000,000 men.

Devastating casualties were brought about by close order fighting and the widespread use of the rifle. The number of casualties led to the increased use of trenches which had previously only been seen in siege warfare.

Robert E. Lee may have waged war in a spirit of chivalry. Generals like Grant and Sherman, however, showed a ruthlessness that was entirely in keeping with the spirit in which modern warfare has come to be waged.

Siege mortars and shells, Virginia.

Left: Confederate troops in action. The South possessed a strong military tradition; southerners had dominated the American army and the cream of its officers resigned in order to serve the Confederacy.

A southern gentleman, accustomed to command, held in common with his soldiers the belief that he could "lick any five Yankees". This spirit enabled the outmanned South to win victory after victory before finally succumbing.

Above: Federal officers grouped around a field gun. The northern soldier was more difficult to train and discipline than the southerner, but he proved to be resourceful and mechanically-minded.

In the early years, he suffered from indecisive command, for northern generals could not match Lee and Jackson. In the stress of war, however, strong commanders like Grant, Sheridan, Thomas and Sherman did emerge.

The Monstrous Ironclads

At Norfolk, Virginia, the Confederates refloated a scuttled Union steam frigate, the *Merrimack*. They cut her hull down to the waterline and built a large cabin sheathed in armour plate and carrying ten guns. Renamed *Virginia*, this ungainly vessel appeared on 8 March 1862 in Hampton Roads where two Union warships, the *Cumberland* and the *Congress*, were blockading the James River. While their fire bounced off her iron sides, *Virginia* closed in and sank both wooden ships. Suddenly it seemed as if the whole naval position had changed. If one ironclad could do such damage, could it not bring an end to the blockade of southern ports and even perhaps bombard Washington and New York?

However, on the day following *Virginia*'s triumph, another ironclad arrived in Hampton Roads. It was the U.S.S. *Monitor* and, at dawn, the two monsters moved to point-blank range and opened fire. As solid shot crashed against the iron plating and ricocheted across the bay, it became clear that neither could seriously hurt the other. *Virginia* twice rammed *Monitor* and only damaged her own prow, but her gunners did make a direct hit on the pilothouse. Around noon, the fight was broken off and *Virginia* steamed back to her base while *Monitor* guarded some stranded Union ships.

Neither vessel ever took part in another battle. *Virginia* was blown up when McClellan captured Norfolk and *Monitor* foundered in a gale some months later.

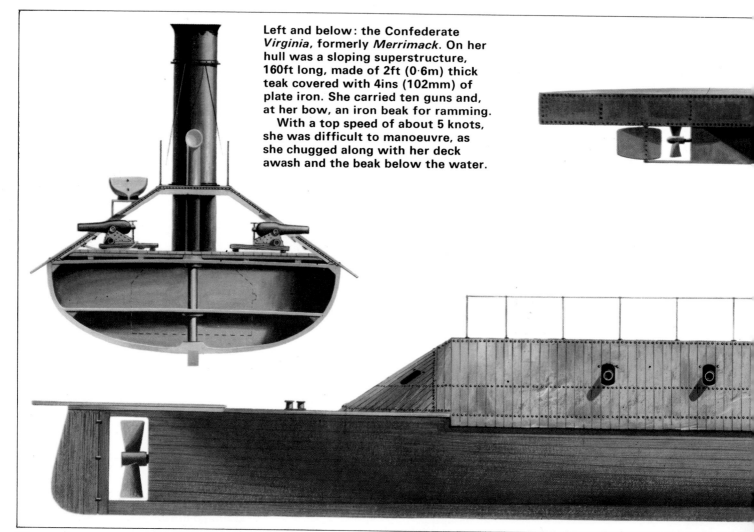

Left and below: the Confederate *Virginia*, formerly *Merrimack*. On her hull was a sloping superstructure, 160ft long, made of 2ft (0·6m) thick teak covered with 4ins (102mm) of plate iron. She carried ten guns and, at her bow, an iron beak for ramming.

With a top speed of about 5 knots, she was difficult to manoeuvre, as she chugged along with her deck awash and the beak below the water.

A sketch of the interior of *Monitor*'s turret with its twin 11-inch guns which could fire in any direction. The guns, like those of *Virginia*, were bottle-shaped muzzle-loaders.

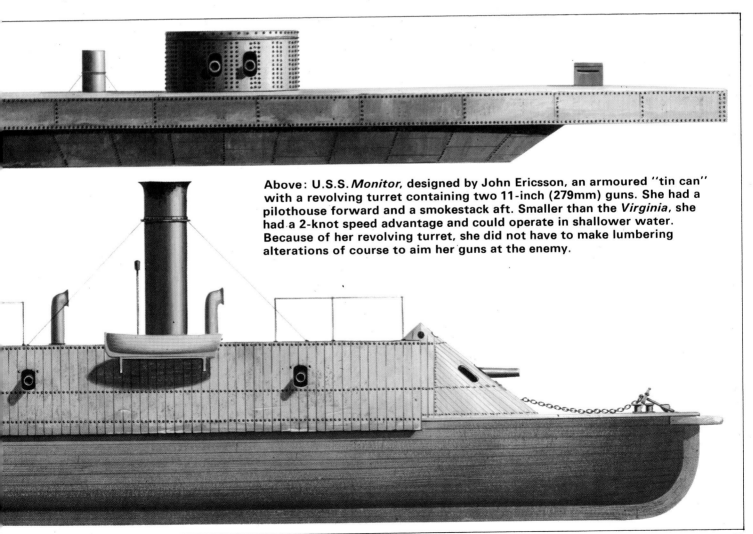

Above: U.S.S. *Monitor*, designed by John Ericsson, an armoured "tin can" with a revolving turret containing two 11-inch (279mm) guns. She had a pilothouse forward and a smokestack aft. Smaller than the *Virginia*, she had a 2-knot speed advantage and could operate in shallower water. Because of her revolving turret, she did not have to make lumbering alterations of course to aim her guns at the enemy.

Battles of the War

In April 1862, McClellan's Union army began the long-delayed march on Richmond but his careful advance was halted when the Confederate general, Joe Johnston, struck hard at Seven Pines. Johnston was wounded and his command passed to Robert E. Lee who counter-attacked by sending Stonewall Jackson to hit the Union forces again and again in the Shenandoah Valley. After J. E. B. Stuart's cavalry had harried McClellan's army, Lee attacked and in the Seven Days Battle, he saved Richmond and inflicted 20,000 casualties on the enemy.

General Pope took over the Union command but Lee beat him decisively at Second Bull Run and Lincoln had to recall McClellan. Lee now marched his ragged army into Maryland, hoping to find food and recruits. The Marylanders provided neither and Lee was lucky to escape severe defeat at Antietam. However, he retreated to Fredericksburg where he smashed General Burnside's assault. In May 1863, at Chancellorsville, Lee won yet another victory, but Jackson was killed.

Meanwhile, in the West, the Confederate Braxton Bragg drove northwards across Kentucky but, in December 1862, he met defeat at Stone's River and reeled back to Chattanooga. Having beaten a Confederate army at Corinth, Ulysses Grant attacked the Confederate stronghold of Vicksburg on the Mississippi river. He captured the town in July 1863.

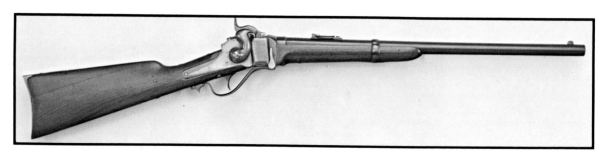

Right: Sharp's New Model Cavalry Carbine, 1863. Some 80,000 of these weapons were purchased by the Union government. The Confederates introduced revolvers.

Confederate dead at Antietam, 17 September 1862, when "Fighting Joe" Hooker almost broke "Stonewall" Jackson's defence.

Lee had crossed into Pennsylvania while Jackson attacked Harper's Ferry. When McClellan appeared with 70,000 men, Jackson had to rush to join Lee at Antietam. In the savage fighting, McClellan should have annihilated the Confederates but Lee managed to extricate his shaken army.

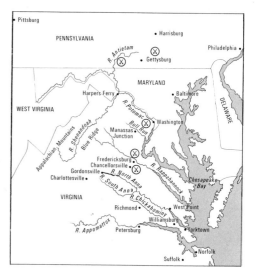

The major battles in the East, 1862–63. After Antietam, Lincoln issued his declaration that all slaves in the rebel states should be free.

This gave a moral uplift to the Unionist cause and had a profound effect abroad. It was now virtually certain that no foreign power would recognize the South.

Above: Fredericksburg, December 1862. Union troops attack the Confederate heights. With the Army of the Potomac, General Burnside moved against Lee who had received reinforcements since Antietam. Burnside made a suicidal frontal assault across a river and up Marye's Heights. He lost 15,000 men.

Below: "Stonewall" Jackson dies at Chancellorsville, May 1863. "Fighting Joe" Hooker, who replaced Burnside, tried to outflank Lee. But Lee sent Jackson on a lightning march to attack the Union right. He succeeded brilliantly but was killed accidentally by his own side. Next day, Lee completed the victory.

The Naval War

When the war opened, Lincoln declared a blockade of southern ports. The Union Navy consisted of only ninety ships, but auxiliary ships were put into service. Northern shipyards built hundreds of new vessels and the North's merchant marine was able to supply trained seamen and officers. The blockade soon became effective in preventing the export of cotton, and the North achieved a decisive success when Admiral Farragut captured New Orleans in 1862.

The Confederacy possessed no navy but blockade-runners were improvised to bring in at least a trickle of supplies. In addition, raiders such as the British-built *Alabama* and *Florida* attacked Northern merchant shipping with some effect. They could not, however, seriously disrupt shipments of wheat and other raw materials to Europe. Inland, on the rivers of the West, Farragut and other commanders gave vital assistance to Union armies. River steamers, protected by heavy timbers, and flat-bottomed paddleships, plated with iron, served as floating artillery whose gunfire played an essential role in reducing Confederate fortifications.

Union ships bombard the forts protecting New Orleans. In a brilliant night action, Farragut forced his way past the defences and sailed upriver to take the city and win control of the lower reaches of the Mississippi.

The wooden ship *Cumberland* is no match for the Confederate ironclad *Virginia* (see page 68). In this period of the naval war, both sides used sailing-ships, steamers and ironclads.

Below: Admiral Farragut on the rigging of his flagship during the Battle of Mobile Bay, August 1864. Ignoring Confederate torpedoes, he put his ships at the head of the line to enter the bay and capture Mobile, the South's second port.

Above: C.S.S. *Nashville*, a Confederate cruiser, destroys the *Harvey Birch*, a three-masted Union merchantman.

Southern blockade-runners carried cotton to neutral ports like Nassau in the Bahamas for shipment to Europe. They returned with much-needed munitions and supplies. Armed cruisers, some of them built in Britain, sank more than 200 northern vessels during the war.

Gettysburg and After

In June 1863, Lee advanced seventy miles north of Washington and Lincoln sent General Meade to intercept him. They met at Gettysburg on 1 July and, after two days of indecisive fighting, Lee sent Pickett to charge up Cemetery Ridge. This was the turning point of the war, for Lee lost a third of his splendid army, a loss he could never make good. But the South fought on. Vicksburg fell, Chattanooga was lost and, in 1864, Grant came east to Virginia to deal hammer blows at Lee. In battles like the Wilderness, Spotsylvania, North Anna and Cold Harbor, Grant's losses were tremendous, but the Union could always find fresh troops. The South could not.

Meanwhile, Sheridan devastated Shenandoah Valley; Sherman took Atlanta and marched through Georgia, destroying everything in his path. When Grant captured Petersburg and the Confederates had to abandon Richmond, Lee knew that the end had come. On 9 April 1865, he surrendered to Grant in McClean's House in the village of Appomattox Court House.

Below: the Battle of Gettysburg: Pickett's immortal charge is halted. Meade, guessing Lee's intention, reinforced his centre with fresh troops and artillery, so Pickett's men charged into a wall of fire.

Destroyed railway lines littered with the remains of a Confederate munitions train. Great areas of the South were reduced to ruins.

The Aftermath of War

At Appomattox, Grant and Lee shook hands and agreed upon an honourable surrender. The aftermath was less honourable.

President Johnson succeeded Lincoln and tried to adopt a moderate policy. He was opposed by a vengeful Congress which imposed "Reconstruction" on the defeated South, dividing it into districts ruled by major-generals.

Political power was handed over to Negroes, to northern fortune-seekers called "carpet-baggers" and to southern allies, known as "scalawags". The impoverished southerners could only nourish their resentment. For a decade, the land was filled with bitterness and hatred.

The murder of President Lincoln in Ford's Theatre, Washington, by John Wilkes Booth, a half-mad southerner: 14 April 1865.

Ex-slaves. Union victory brought freedom—of a kind.

Lincoln's Death

Just five days after Appomattox, Lincoln was murdered in Washington. By that deed, Booth removed the one man who would have treated the South with "malice toward none, with charity for all".

In Abraham Lincoln, the war produced America's greatest hero. At first, hardly anyone realized the true stature of this gaunt homely lawyer. As the struggle wore on, however, men came to appreciate his patience, wisdom and generosity of spirit. He never appealed to prejudice or uttered one vindictive word against the southerners.

As one war veteran said, "Take him altogether, he was the best man this country ever produced."

Slavery Abolished

Southern slaves were freed in 1865 and, by the Fifteenth Amendment to the Constitution, they gained the right to vote. In all ex-Confederate states, except Georgia, white voters were outnumbered by Negroes. But the Negroes' vote was manipulated by corrupt politicians. The whites gradually regained control by political activity and through terrorism exerted by the Ku-Klux-Klan, a secret society.

Throughout the South, the freed blacks were reduced to a state of subservience not far removed from slavery

The Cowboy's Life

The Spanish had raised cattle in the South-West for centuries and, after Texas was annexed in 1845, American ranchers bred a tough lean animal that thrived on the grassy plains. The biggest problem was to get the cattle to market. In the 1850's, ranchers began driving their steers overland, even westwards all the way to California. During the Civil War, the drives were halted. When peace came, however, new trails were made across the open range to railheads like Abilene and Dodge City, whence hundreds of thousands of longhorns were transported to the stockyards of the East.

The cowboys who made the "long drives" became an American legend—heroes in chaps and five-gallon hats who sang on the lonely trail and shot it out with rustlers and Indians. Their hey-day lasted only twenty years, from 1865 to 1885. Destruction of the buffalo herds left the limitless plains to ranchers until the advance of farming and barbed wire pushed the open range farther and farther west. When the terrible winter of 1885 killed the feed and most of the cattle, the cowboys' golden era came to an end.

A frontiersman with his six-shooter. Americans then cherished their constitutional right to bear arms, as some still do. In the Wild West, every cowboy carried a pair of Colt revolvers for use against Indians, rustlers and sheepmen whose flocks cropped the precious grass.

"Peacemaker" Colt revolver of 1873, also known as the "Frontier Six-Shooter". Still in production, this was the best known gun of the American West, a single action, six-shot, gate-loaded revolver, made in twenty different calibres and five barrel-lengths.

Right: an advertisement for Buffalo Bill's Wild West Show, first organized in 1883. As the white man moved west and the railroads extended across the plains, former soldiers and professional hunters were employed to exterminate the vast herds of bison or buffaloes.

Colonel W. F. "Buffalo Bill" Cody, who made a reputation as a marksman, claimed to have killed 4,280 bison in 18 months. By 1885, these great animals, which had provided the Indians with food, robes and tent materials, were practically extinct.

Cody later became a showman, touring with a troupe of cowboys.

Cowboys hunting wild horses along the trail—from an oil-painting by Charles Russell.

The Cattle Trails

After the Civil War, cattle were driven into Missouri up the Sedalia Trail. Later, an Illinois cattleman named McCoy set up pens, stables and hotels at Abilene to make it a great cattle terminal. Abilene handled 700,000 cattle in 1871. The railway extended westward and new cow towns took over the leadership: Ellsworth, Dodge City and Cheyenne.

On the "long drives", lasting two months or more, half a dozen cowboys, each with pony, lariat and six-shooter, would control a thousand half-wild steers. The animals grazed on the march but they fed mainly at night, while cowboys rode about the herd, singing to the cattle to keep them together.

At the end of the drive, after weeks of spending fifteen to eighteen hours in the saddle, the cowhands were paid off. They often spent their pay in a few days, "painting the town red".

Drunk on fiery whisky, they would ride about the town and into saloons, firing their pistols in light-hearted devilry. Sometimes they would pay off scores against rival ranches. When the spree was over, they signed on again for another hard spell in the saddle.

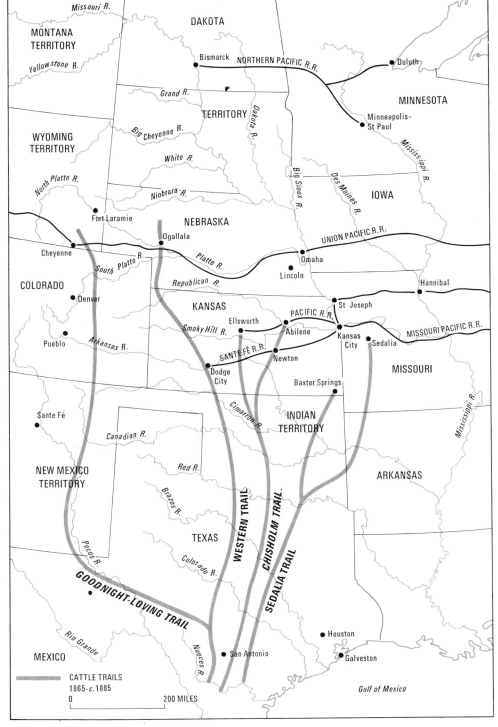

A camp on the trail, with chuck-wagon carrying the cowboys' rations.

Left: the four great cattle trails which had to take more westerly roads as the open range was settled by farmers.

The American Indian

Covered wagons, gold rushes, cattle trails and the white man's movement into the West all threatened the Indian way of life. As farming opened up the lands west of the Mississippi, tribes were pushed into the territories of the Plains Indians. Some tribes came to agreement with the white men, others resisted fiercely. All came to realize that treaties and agreements usually proved worthless, especially if gold should be discovered on land granted to the Indians.

In 1864, occurred the Sand Creek Massacre when several hundred Cheyenne were killed by men of the Colorado Militia. This led to open warfare, followed by further treaties and renewed betrayals. Given a reservation in Dakota, the Sioux were angered when prospectors came flooding in after gold. In 1876, George A. Custer and a detachment of American troops were wiped out at Little Big Horn. Massive retaliation brought defeat to the Sioux, and relentless pressure broke the resistance of north-western tribes, the Blackfeet, the Comanches and the fierce Apaches. The final act of violence was the slaughter of three hundred Sioux at Wounded Knee in 1891.

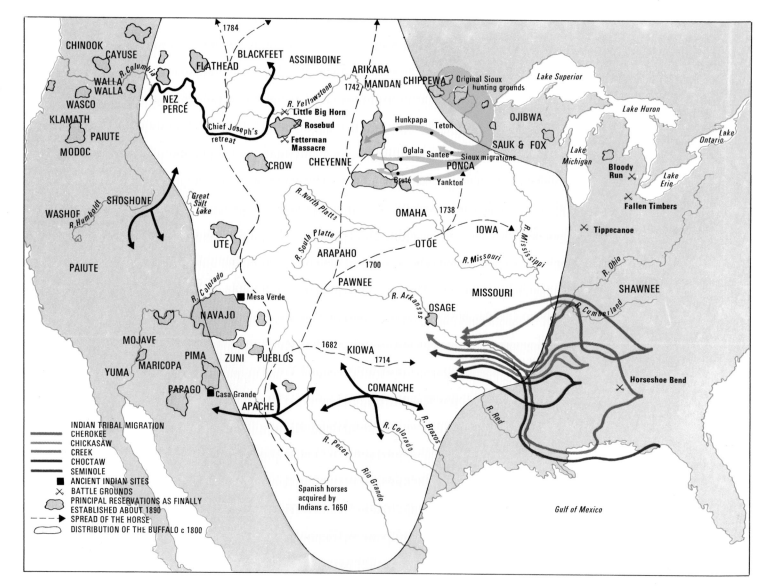

Map showing the main Indian tribes with their areas of settlement. Notice the small reservations, the migrations of the Sioux in the north and of eastern tribes forced westwards across the Mississippi. These migrations added pressure to the Plains Indians' hunting range and led to inter-tribal warfare.

The Spaniards first introduced the horse into America. The Indians became expert horsemen and their hunting ability advanced. The buffalo herds had become smaller even before white men destroyed them.

Geronimo, the last great Apache chief, surrenders to General Crook, 1886. He was sent into exile in Florida and never allowed to return to his Apache homeland.

An Indian chief. Among the more warlike tribes were the Blackfeet, Crows, Cheyennes and Sioux of the Plains, the Comanches of the central areas. To the south-west, rode the fierce Navajos and Apaches. Led by warriors like Sitting Bull, Crazy Horse, Black Kettle, Red Cloud and Geronimo, they were a match for the best cavalry in the world.

Left: Indians attack a construction gang in Kansas. The railway is being built on tribal hunting-grounds.

The Indian Tragedy

As pioneer settlers, ranchers and miners moved into the last great areas left to the Indians, conflict was inevitable.

Land-hungry Americans could not bear the prospect of nomadic tribes occupying thousands of square miles of fertile land. They adopted a policy of herding the tribes into smaller and smaller reservations.

Yet even the reservations were violated. The Sioux were granted the Black Hills of Dakota for "as long as the sun shall rise and the rivers shall run". Yet this did not stop white men entering their territory when gold was discovered in the hills.

The buffalo was essential to Indian life but the vast herds were a menace to farmers and railroads, so they had to be wiped out.

The Dawes Act of 1887 aimed to teach Indians agriculture and the white man's values. Yet it pushed them into desolate areas, like the Navajo reservation in Utah. This treatment led to a loss of Indian dignity and self-respect. They became a broken people.

Left: buffalo hunters. The hides were sold for leather. In 1872–4, the slaughter reached three million.

America Expands

The years following the Civil War saw the spectacular expansion of American industry and agriculture. No other country grew so rapidly in wealth, numbers and strength. Between 1865 and 1900, the population more than doubled and the United States became the world's leading industrial power. It stood first in the production of manufactured goods, in its output of iron and steel, in railroad mileage, telegraph and telephone lines and in the production of gold, petroleum, coal, copper, cattle, cotton, corn and wheat.

This remarkable expansion was due to America's ability to exploit her natural riches through improved railway communications, the growth of industrial cities and settlement of the West. The millions of immigrants who arrived were prepared to work for low wages, and ruthlessly efficient business methods emerged.

Expansion led to increase of exports, so it became necessary for America to set up a trading network and protect her interests. By the end of the century, she had become a world power with an empire in the Pacific.

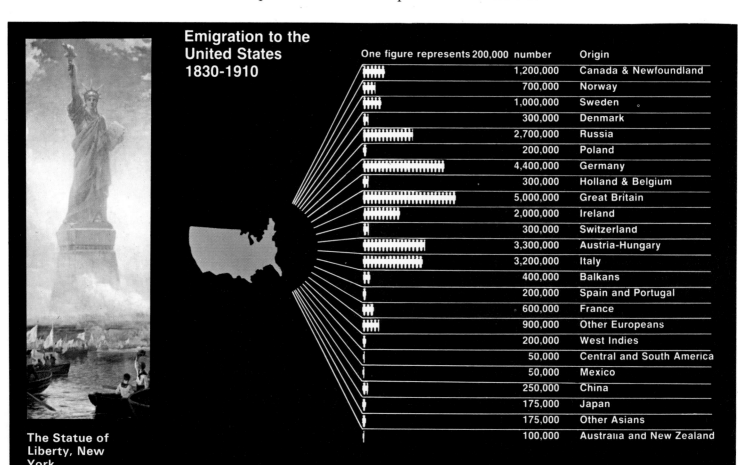

Emigration to the United States 1830-1910

One figure represents 200,000

number	Origin
1,200,000	Canada & Newfoundland
700,000	Norway
1,000,000	Sweden
300,000	Denmark
2,700,000	Russia
200,000	Poland
4,400,000	Germany
300,000	Holland & Belgium
5,000,000	Great Britain
2,000,000	Ireland
300,000	Switzerland
3,300,000	Austria-Hungary
3,200,000	Italy
400,000	Balkans
200,000	Spain and Portugal
600,000	France
900,000	Other Europeans
200,000	West Indies
50,000	Central and South America
50,000	Mexico
250,000	China
175,000	Japan
175,000	Other Asians
100,000	Australia and New Zealand

The Statue of Liberty, New York.

The New Immigrants

Millions of immigrants poured into the United States between 1870 and 1900. Most were ill-educated and unskilled. A quarter of them came from eastern and southern Europe—Jews, Poles, Czechs, Serbs, Croats, Turks, Greeks and Italians.

Many native-born Americans were alarmed by these hordes of poor people with their strange ideas and customs. They were ready to work long hours for low wages, and were resented by the newly-formed trade unions for they kept wages down.

They settled chiefly in the industrial North-East and in the Pacific states where they lived in the poorest areas of the great cities. Yet America's dramatic expansion could not have taken place without them, and their children absorbed America's culture and ideals with remarkable speed.

An American express in about 1850. By the 1880's, five main lines crossed the continent, while every part of the Mississippi Valley and the East was linked by railways. Capitalists like Vanderbilt and J. P. Morgan made fortunes out of the railway companies.

Big Business

A marked feature of the American scene was the development of "big business" methods. Astute men saw that the best way to cut costs and avoid competition was to form giant corporations (also called "pools" or "trusts") to buy up or crush rival firms. It was then possible to control prices and fix profits.

Famous "captains of industry" included John D. Rockefeller, the oil magnate, Andrew Carnegie, steel, and J. Pierpont Morgan and Cornelius Vanderbilt, railways. The Duke family controlled tobacco, the Guggenheims, copper, while Philip Armour ruled the meat industry.

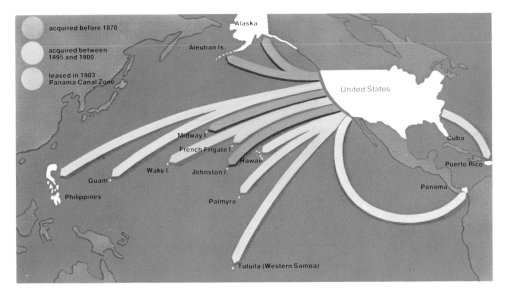

The growth of America's empire. Her new island bases enabled her to dominate the Pacific. The Panama Canal was started in 1905.

An Alaskan native. Seward's purchase of Alaska was ridiculed until its enormous riches became apparent.

A World Power

William Henry Seward, Secretary of State from 1861–1869, was the first American statesman to see that the United States would expand beyond its existing borders.

He wanted bases in the Pacific and Caribbean to protect trade, and, in 1867, he obtained Midway Island, lying west of Hawaii. He also bought Alaska from Russia.

During the next two decades, American business interests were actively pursued in South America, China and Hawaii.

When, in 1895, Cuba rose against its Spanish rulers, American sympathy and self-interest led to a brief war. In 1898, the U.S. battleship *Maine* was blown up in Havana Harbour. War was declared and the United States defeated Spain in little more than three months.

By the peace treaty, Cuba gained its independence with close political and commercial ties with America. In addition, Puerto Rico was annexed, along with the Pacific island of Guam and the Philippines, where local patriots put up a lively resistance.

The Republic of Hawaii was annexed in 1898, and it provided the American Navy with a magnificent anchorage at Pearl Harbour.

To its own surprise, the United States found that it had acquired an overseas empire.

Defeat of the Spanish Fleet at Manila Bay in the Philippines by Commodore Dewey. Admiral Sampson destroyed another Spanish fleet in Cuba.

Scramble for Africa

Britain had bought Cape Colony in 1815 in order to obtain a calling-place for ships going to India. The Dutch or Boer farmers resented British rule and in 1836 they made the Great Trek northwards to found the Orange Free State and Transvaal. In face of Zulu hostility, these republics were annexed by Britain in 1877, but they recovered their independence after defeating a British force at Majuba Hill in 1881.

Britain's Suez Canal shares involved her in Egypt. After some fighting in support of the *Khedive* (Viceroy) against an army mutiny, the British took virtual control of the country. Egypt's rebellious province, the Sudan, was recovered by General Kitchener at the Battle of Omdurman.

Meanwhile, missionaries and explorers, like Livingstone and Stanley, had opened Europe's eyes to the continent's riches. In the scramble for Africa, most of the Powers acquired extensive territories, but the lion's share fell to Britain. Not only did she strengthen her possessions in West and East Africa, but, thanks to Cecil Rhodes, she gained a vast new country, given the name of Rhodesia, in 1895.

David Livingstone, 1813–73.

Livingstone gathered a vast amount of information about Africa during his travels (1843–73). He travelled the length of the Zambesi and discovered Victoria Falls and Lake Nyasa. The public was thrilled by his discoveries, yet he considered himself more a missionary than an explorer, and was embarrassed by his own fame. He disappeared in 1871, and the *New York Herald* sent H. M. Stanley to find him. Their now famous meeting at Ujiji led to further exploration, with the two men working together. Stanley himself later explored the Congo for King Leopold of Belgium.

Above: a Zulu *impi* or company of warriors ready for battle. Under their famous chief, Cetewayo, the Zulus dramatically defeated a British force at Isandhlwana (1879), but their power was broken at Ulundi.

Below: British charge at Omdurman, 1898. Kitchener advanced slowly into the Sudan, taking nearly three years to reach Khartoum before he destroyed the army of the Dervish leader, the *Mahdi*.

Left: Scottish soldiers after the victory of Tel-el-Kebir, 1882, when Sir Garnet Wolseley defeated Arabi Pasha, leader of a mutiny against the Khedive, ruler of Egypt.

Below: map of Africa showing how the European powers divided the continent among themselves, leaving only Liberia and Ethiopia free from foreign rule or "protection".

After the Conference of Berlin (1884), called by Bismarck, the German Chancellor, each nation was awarded its "spheres of influence".

Spain acquired a strip in the north-east, Italy a tract by the Red Sea. France claimed the Sahara and Algeria. Germany and Portugal gained territories on both the east and west coasts. Belgium founded the Congo Free State and Britain took nearly all the rest.

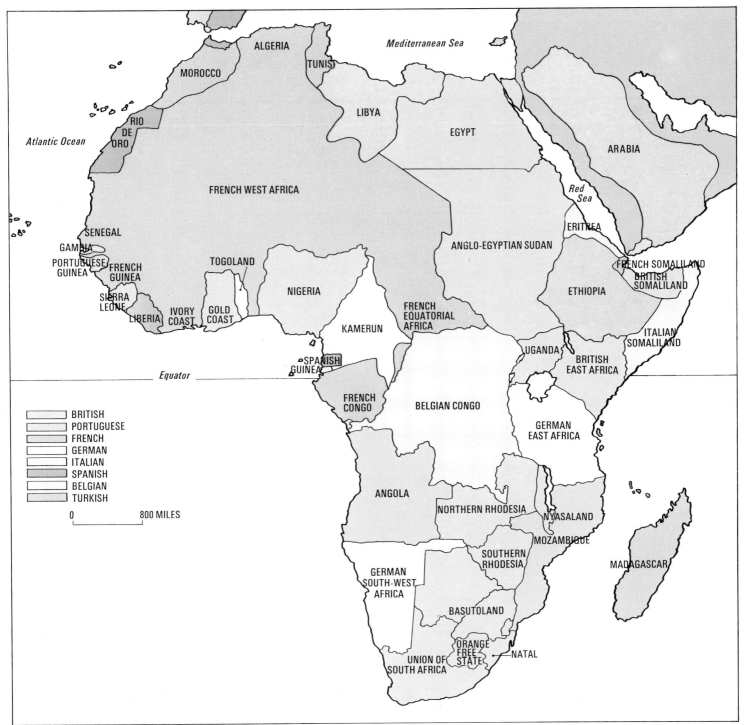

South Africa

After the British had defeated the Zulus, the Transvaal Boers demanded the return of their independence which Gladstone agreed to in 1881. However, the British retained an overlordship which the Boers resented. When gold was discovered, hordes of outsiders, *Uitlanders*, poured into the Transvaal, completely outnumbering the Boers. These Uitlanders soon found themselves paying heavy taxes to the Boer government without receiving any civic rights. The situation became so explosive that a plot was launched for an uprising. Cecil Rhodes, Prime Minister of the Cape, promised to send armed support to the Uitlanders and, in 1895, Dr Jameson crossed into the Transvaal with a small force. However, no rising took place and the Jameson Raid was a fiasco.

Ill-feeling persisted and the Uitlanders petitioned the British Government to intervene on their behalf. When troop reinforcements were ordered to the Cape, Transvaal's President Kruger demanded their recall. This was not forthcoming and, in October 1899, the two Boer republics declared war on Britain. At the outset, the Boers held all the trump cards—superior numbers, modern German artillery and knowledge of the country. The British suffered some sharp reverses before good generalship and greater resources brought victory.

Sorting Kimberley diamonds. Their discovery brought prospectors pouring into Orange Free State.

Cecil Rhodes, the clergyman's son who made a fortune from diamonds. He held a vision of British supremacy from the Cape to Cairo.

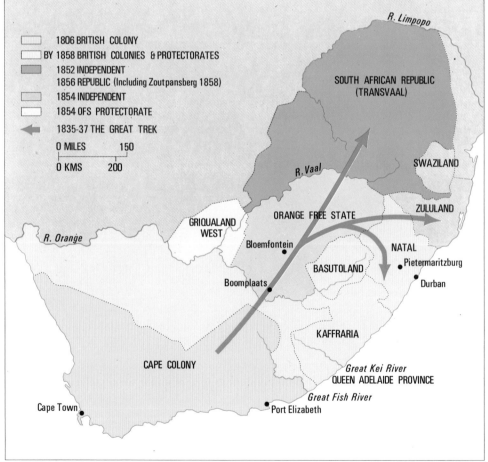

Map showing the two Boer republics and British colonies in South Africa in 1858, 40 years before the war.

Dissatisfaction with British rule had caused Boers to make the Great Trek from Cape Colony in the 1830's.

They went in ox-wagons, driving their cattle before them. They crossed the Orange river and the Vaal to found their two republics. They also established Natal which the British annexed in 1845.

Paul Kruger (1825–1904), President of the Transvaal. "Oom Paul", as he was called, made the Great Trek as a boy and became implacably hostile to the British.

Preparing for war, he bought large quantities of arms from Germany. In 1900, he fled to Europe to seek alliances against Britain.

Boer soldiers await action at Spion Kop where the British suffered a bloody defeat. The Boers were fine riders and marksmen.

Royal Horse Artillery cross a river under fire. Khaki uniforms were issued to match the terrain.

The Boer War, 1899–1902

The war fell into three stages. The first months were marked by defeats for the British under Sir Redvers Buller. The Boers might have swept through Cape Colony, but instead they besieged garrisons at Ladysmith, Kimberley and Mafeking.

In February 1900, Lord Roberts arrived, with Kitchener as Chief of Staff, in command of large reinforcements. The besieged garrisons were relieved, and the main Boer army under Cronje was defeated at Paardeberg. The British also took Bloemfontein and knocked the Orange Free State out of the war. With the capture of Pretoria and the defeat of Botha's Boer army at Bergensdal, Kruger fled and the British annexed the Transvaal.

The last phase lasted from November 1900 to May 1902. Boer commandos waged a long guerilla war under the leadership of Smuts, Botha, De Wet, Hertzog and others. It was a bitter struggle; Kitchener placed Boer civilians in concentration camps and destroyed farms.

The Boers finally conceded defeat at the Treaty of Vereeniging in 1902. The Boer republics became British colonies but they were promised eventual self-government. This was granted in 1906.

Boer War medals with heads of Edward VII and Queen Victoria, for the Queen died before the end of the war. The British lost more men from disease, mainly enteric fever, than in action.

85

Time Chart: the main events in world history

British Isles and Ireland

During this century, Britain advanced to a position of great power and influence. There were, nevertheless, considerable economic ups and downs and political agitation. Unrest was particularly acute in Ireland, where Gladstone failed to bring in Home Rule. It was an age of social and political reform, of imperial expansion and literary achievement.

Europe

The forces of liberalism and nationalism struggled against the old empires of Austria, Turkey and Russia. The new nations of Greece, Germany and Italy emerged.

	British Isles and Ireland	Europe
1815	Widespread distress; Spa Fields Riot; Peterloo Massacre (1819). Six Acts passed. Accession of George IV (1820). Cato Street Conspiracy. Repeal of Combination Acts. Formation of Catholic Association in Ireland. Literature: Austen, Scott, Byron, Keats, Shelley. Art: Turner, Constable. Science: Faraday.	Allied armies left France. Greek War of Independence (1821–30). Liberal regimes in Spain and Portugal snuffed out. Austria dominated Italy and Germany. Metternich, Austrian Chancellor, led European diplomacy. Literature: de Vigny, Lamartine, Heine. Music: Beethoven, Schubert.
1825	Catholic Emancipation in Ireland. Metropolitan Police Force founded. Stockton–Darlington Railway. Stephenson's *Rocket*. Accession of William IV (1830). Bristol Riots. Reform Act of 1832 extends vote to middle classes. Factory Act. Tolpuddle Martyrs. Abolition of slavery in British possessions (1833). Essayist: Cobbett. Literature: Tennyson.	July Revolution in France (1830); Charles X deposed; liberal monarchy of Louis Philippe. Greece became independent. Civil war in Spain and Portugal. Mazzini led risings in Italy. Literature: Hugo, Balzac, Stendhal. Music: Rossini, Mendelssohn.
1835	Accession of Queen Victoria (1837). Foundation of Anti-Corn Law League. Chartist riots, demands for greater political freedom. Employment of women and children in mines forbidden. Rowland Hill's Penny Post introduced. Great railway boom. Literature: Carlyle, Dickens, Macaulay, Hood.	Anglo-French rivalry in Mediterranean and Near East. Tsar Nicholas I of Russia active in European affairs. Industrialization of western Europe. Art: Delacroix, Corot. Music: Berlioz, Wagner, Verdi.
1845	Potato famine in Ireland. Young Ireland movement. Corn Laws repealed (1846). Great Chartist petition failed (1848). Palmerston Foreign Secretary. Don Pacifico affair. Great Exhibition (1851). Literature: Browning, Disraeli, Thackeray, Brontës. Art: Pre-Raphaelites.	1848 Year of Revolutions; France (Louis Philippe ousted), Italy, Germany, Austria, Hungary, Spain. Failure of national uprisings. Napoleon III became Emperor of France (1851). Crimean War (1854–55). Literature: Dostoievsky, Dumas, Turgenev. Music: Brahms, Liszt.
1855	Death of Prince Albert (1861). Commercial Treaty with France. Palmerston Prime Minister during Crimean War. Gladstone's Free Trade policy. Bessemer converter introduced in steel industry. Atlantic cable laid. Literature: Trollope, Eliot, Kingsley. Music: Hallé concerts. Art: Frith.	Treaty of Paris ended Crimean War (1856). Orsini plot to murder Napoleon III. War between Austria and Sardinia; Garibaldi's uprising; Kingdom of Italy proclaimed (1861). Austria and Prussia at war with Denmark. Literature: Flaubert. Art: Degas, Manet. Science: Pasteur.
1865	Second Reform Act (1867) extended franchise further. Fenian uprising failed in Ireland. Fenian outrages in England. Gladstone's Irish Land Act. Disestablishment of the Irish Church. Education Act (1870). Disraeli Prime Minister (1874). Cardwell's Army Reforms. Literature: Lewis Carroll, Meredith.	War between Austria and Italy; Venetia ceded to Italy. Austro-Prussian War (1866). Franco-Prussian War (1870); France defeated; Napoleon III abdicated. Bismarck unified Germany (1871). Politics: Karl Marx *Das Kapital*. Art: birth of Impressionism; Renoir, Monet.
1875	Public Health Act. Victoria proclaimed Empress of India. Disraeli bought Suez Canal shares. Irish M.P.'s obstructed Parliament. Irish Land League formed; boycotting; Parnell imprisoned; Cavendish murdered. Red Flag Act restricted road speeds to 4 m.p.h. Parsons' steam turbine. Literature: Hardy, Stevenson. Music: Gilbert and Sullivan.	Period of German dominance and French weakness. Carlists defeated in Spain. Turkish Bulgarian atrocities. Congress of Berlin (1878). Triple Alliance of Germany, Austria and Italy. Literature: Ibsen. Art: Cézanne. Music: Grieg, Tschaikovsky.
1885	Gladstone's Irish Home Rule Bill defeated. Fall of Parnell. Great London Dock Strike. Keir Hardie elected M.P. Agricultural depression. Jack the Ripper murdered six women (1888). Rover safety bicycle. First electric tramcar. Dunlop's pneumatic tyre. First underground railway. Literature: Shaw, Yeats, Kipling. Art: Burne-Jones.	Serbo-Bulgarian War. Austro-Russian tension. Franco-Russian agreement. Accession of Kaiser William II; fall of Bismarck. Kiel Canal completed. Dreyfus case in France. Benz, Daimler, first motor-cars; X-rays discovered; Lumière invented cinematograph. Literature: Zola. Art: Gaugin, Van Gogh.
1895 **1901**	Economic depression. Taff Vale Case. Troops sent to South Africa. Death of Queen Victoria. Marconi demonstrated wireless telegraphy. Anglo-German tension.	Dreyfus refused new trial (1895). Expansion of German navy. Unrest in the Balkans. Hague Peace Conference.

Asia and Australia

Most of India came under British control. China was exploited by the colonial powers. Japan became a world power; Australia and New Zealand became nations.

Tsar Alexander I returned to repressive policies in Russia.
Lachlan Macquarie became Governor of New South Wales.
Britain acquired Singapore.
First Burmese War (1824); Rangoon taken.

Mehemet Ali defeated Sultan of Turkey in Asia Minor.
Colonization of Western Australia. Sturt explored Murray River.
Illicit trade in Indian opium in China.
Lord William Bentinck, Governor General, introduced reforms in India.

British occupied Aden.
Founding of Southern Australia; settlement of Victoria.
New Zealand Association formed.
First Afghan War (1838–42).
First Opium War (1839–42); Treaty of Nanking, China ceded Hong Kong.

Leichhardt explored Northern Australia.
Sikh Wars (from 1845); Punjab annexed.
Second Burmese War (1852).
First Maori War (1843–48).
Convicts sent to Western Australia. Australian Colonies Government Act. Gold rush in Victoria.
Japan and U.S. made trade treaty.

Oudh annexed. Indian Mutiny (1857).
Government of India Act.
Chinese ports opened to foreign powers.
Peking captured by British and French.
Burke-Wills expedition in Australia.
Opening of Siam to trade.
Tai Ping rebellion in China.

French in Cambodia and Indo-China.
End of British East India Company.
Opening of Suez Canal (1869).
India's trade increased.
Dowager Empress Tzu Hsi ruled China.
Annexation of Fiji.

Russia invaded Turkey (1877).
Second Afghan War (1878–80)
Vast volcanic explosion at Krakatoa, Java.
Foreign powers obtained further trading rights in China.
Meiji period in Japan, growth of industry and spread of western ideas.

Powers fixed "spheres of influence" in Pacific.
First meeting of Indian National Congress (1885). Upper Burma annexed by British (1886).
Young Turk Movement formed (1891).
Trans-Siberian railway completed in Russia.
Gold found in Western Australia; gold rush.
China and Japan at war (1894).

Japan dominated Korea. Scramble for concessions in China. Tzu Hsi repressed reform; Boxer Rebellion against colonial powers (1900).
Commonwealth of Australia founded (1900).

Africa

As explorers revealed Africa's riches, the European powers scrambled to divide her. Britain gained the lion's share, but opposition in South Africa led to the Boer War.

Gold Coast became a British colony.
First Ashanti War began (1823).
British immigrants in Cape Colony.
Egypt rule by Mehemet Ali, Sudan conquered.
Foundation of Liberian Republic for freed American slaves. (1820).

Cape Colony extended to Orange River.
Laing crossed Sahara desert from Tripoli to Timbuktu.
French took Algiers.
British occupied Mombassa.
Abolition of slavery (1833) angered Boer settlers in Cape Colony.

The Great Trek by Boer farmers (1836).
Natal founded (1840).
Zulus defeated by Boers at Blood River.
Gambia made a British colony.
Natal annexed by Britain (1843).
Creation of Basutoland.
French at war with Morocco.

Kaffir War on borders of Cape Colony.
Livingstone crossed Kalahari desert; discovered Victoria Falls.
Growing hostility between British and Boers in South Africa.
British recognized independence of Transvaal.

Transvaal organized as Boer state; Pretoria founded. Indian labourers imported into Natal.
British explorers, Burton and Speke, discovered Lake Tanganyika.
Speke, Grant, Baker explored headwaters of the Nile.

Suez Canal opened.
Diamonds discovered in Orange Free State.
Kimberley founded.
Death of Livingstone. Stanley explored Central Africa
General Gordon, governor of Sudan.
Second Ashanti War (1873–74).

Anglo-Portuguese dispute over Delagoa Bay.
Transvaal annexed; Zulu War (1879).
Boers defeated British at Majuba Hill.
Scramble for Africa: French invaded Tunis; British bombarded Alexandria.
Stanley explored upper Congo.
Gordon arrived at Khartoum (1884).

Death of Gordon at Khartoum (1885).
Southern Nigeria annexed. Uganda annexed (1890); British East Africa Co. formed.
Rhodesia founded.
Suez Canal opened to all nations.
French advanced in West Africa.

Jameson Raid (1896).
Ethiopians defeated Italians at Adowa (1896).
Battle of Omdurman (1898).
Outbreak of Boer War (1899).

The Americas

Despite the agony of the Civil War, the U.S. grew rapidly, settling the West, producing enormous wealth and acquiring an empire. South America broke free from colonial rule.

Argentina, Brazil, Costa Rica, Mexico, Peru all declared themselves independent.
Florida ceded to United States.
Bolivar drove Spanish out of Peru.
Monroe Doctrine proclaimed (1823); beginnings of American foreign policy established.

Erie Canal completed.
Settlement of mid-West began.
Andrew Jackson, President of United States (1829–37); era of social reform.
First railway built in United States.
Beginnings of anti-slavery movement.

Texas became a republic (1836); siege of the *Alamo*.
Financial crisis in United States (1837).
Dispute between United States and Canada; rebellion in Canada. Durham Report (1839) resulted in Canadian Act of Union.

Texas annexed by United States (1845).
Oregon Treaty between Britain and United States (1846). Mexican War; U.S. gained New Mexico, California.
Gold discovered in California; gold rush.
Mormons settled in Utah.
Literature: Melville, Harriet Beecher Stowe.

John Brown's raid on Harper's Ferry.
Lincoln elected President (1861).
Southern States formed Confederacy.
Civil War (1861–65); Bull Run (1861), Antietam, Chancellorsville, Gettysburg (1863).

Lee surrendered at Appomattox.
Assassination of Lincoln (1865).
Slavery abolished. Alaska purchased from Russia (1867).
Treaty of Washington with Britain.
Dominion of Canada founded (1867).
Literature: Walt Whitman, Longfellow.

Indian Wars: Battle of Little Big Horn.
Apache rising.
Great railway strike in United States.
Cuba revolted against Spanish rule.
Panama Canal begun.
United States acquired Pearl Harbour.
Literature: Mark Twain, Henry James.

American Federation of Labour formed.
United States obtained control of Hawaii.
Settlement of the West.
First Pan-American Conference.
Edison's electric lamp; Ford's first car; moving pictures shown in New York.

Spanish-American War (1898); Cuba independent. United States acquired Philippines.
Klondyke gold rush.
President McKinley assassinated.

Index

Lee, General Robert E., **66**, 67, 70–1, 74–5
leisure, 14–15, **14–15**, 42, *see also* entertainment, sport
Lewis, Meriewether, explorer, 59
Liberal Party, British, 31, 45
Lilienthal, aircraft pioneer, 12
Lincoln, Abraham, president of United States, 63–5, 70, 72, 74–5, **75**
Lister, Joseph, scientist, 35
literature, *see* writers
Little Big Horn, battle of, 78
Liverpool, 35, 47
Livingstone, David, explorer, 82, **82**
Louisiana, 58, 61, **62**, 65

McAdam, John L., engineer, 16
Macdonald, John, prime minister of Canada, 51
McClellan, General George, 65–6, **66**, 68, 70
McCormick, Cyrus, inventor, 60
machines, *see* industry, inventions, agriculture
Madox Brown, Ford, artist, 2, **2**, 22, **23**, 29
Mafeking, 85
Mahdi, the, 82
mail, 8, 13, 53, 57, 86
Malta, 6, **7**
Manchester, 30, 35
Manila Bay, battle of, 81
Mann, Tom, trade unionist, 32
Maoris, 48–9, **49**
Maritime Provinces, *see* Canada
Marshalsea, debtors' prison, 39
Marx, Karl, 32
Maryland, 63, 65, 70
Mauritius, 6, **7**
medicine, 36, *see also* health, hospitals
Melbourne, Lord, British prime minister, **5**
merchant navy, British, 18
Meredith, George, novelist, 42
Metropolitan Line, **17**
Metropolitan Police, 38–9, **39**, 86
Metternich, Austrian leader, 4
Mexico, war with United States, 58–9, **59**
microphone, 13
middle class, the, 35; at home, 10–11, **10–11**, 40–1, **40**; in India, **7**; and the vote, 30
Millais, Sir John, artist, 29
mining, *see* industry
Mississippi river, 57, **57**, **61**, 72, 81
Mississippi, state of, 65–6
Missouri, state of, 65, 77
Mobile Bay, battle of, **73**
Morgan, J. Pierpoint, American railwayman, 81
Munroe, James, president of United States, 59, **59**
Morris, William, artist, 21–3, **23**
Morse, Samuel, **12**
motor car, 12, 16
motor cycle, 16
Mudki, battle of, 53, **53**
Majuba Hill, battle of, 82
music-hall, 14–15

nannie, the Victorian, **10**, 40–1
Napoleon Bonaparte, 4
Napoleon III, 54–5, **55**
Napoleonic Wars, 4, 6, 24, 59
Nasmyth, James, inventor, 20
Natal, 84, **84**
navy; British, 6; American, 81; Spanish, 81, *see also* merchant navy, American Civil War
Negroes, 75, **75**, *see also* slavery
Newgate Prison, **39**
New Mexico, 58–9, 62
New Orleans, 66, 72, **72**; battle of, 59

newspapers, 14
New York Journal, the, 43, **43**
New Zealand, 6, 24, 26, 47–8, **48–9**
Nightingale, Florence, nurse, 37, **37**, 54
nursing, 35–6, **36**

O'Connor, Feargus, Chartist, 30
Omdurman, battle of, 82, **82**
omnibus, 16, **17**
Ontario, *see* Canada
Orange Free State, 82, **83**, 84–5, **84**
Owen, Robert, 32

Paardeburg, battle of, 85
Pacific Railway, **9**
Palmerston, Lord, British prime minister, 86
Papineau, Louis, Canadian rebel leader, 50
parliamentary reform, 4–5, **5**, 30–1, **30–1**, *see also* Houses of Parliament
Parnell, Charles Stuart, 44, **44**
Parsons, Charles A., inventor, 20
Pasteur, Louis, 35
Paxton, Joseph, architect, 221
Pearl Harbour, 81
Peel, Sir Robert, British home secretary, 38–9, **39**
"Peelers", *see* Metropolitan Police
Penny Black, stamp, **13**
"People's Charter", the, 30
Peterloo massacre, the, 5, **5**, 86
Phillipines, 81
phonograph, *see* gramophone
photography, 12–13, **13**, 43, **43**, 54–5
Pitt, William (the Younger), British prime minister, 32
police, *see* Metropolitan Police
Polk, James, president of United States, 59
poor, *see* poverty, Poor Law
Poor Law, 34
population, and birth control; in Britain, 2, 10, 34, 36, **36**; in America, 58, **58**, 80, **80**
post, *see* mail
potato famine, 36, 44–5, 86
Potter, Beatrix, writer, 40
poverty, **2**, 3, **18**, 36; and reforms, 34–5, **34–5**; *see also* farm labourers, dockers, Ireland
Pre-Raphaelites, the, 28–9, 86
printing, 28, 40
prisons, 35, 39, **39**
Puerto Rico, 81
Punjab, 6, **52**, 53, **53**

Quebec, *see* Canada

Radicals, 5, **5**
radio, 12
Raffles, Stamford, 6
Ragged schools, 34, **41**
railways, 2, 8–9, **8–9**; electricity in, 12, 17; mail carried by, 8, 13; and holidays, 14; underground, 16, **17**; steam, 17, **28**; manufacturing works, **19**; networks, 19, 24, 52–3; engineering, 20; stations, **9**, 22, **53**; *see also* United States
Red Cloud, Indian chief, 79
reform, *see* education, health, housing, parliament, industry, trade unions
Reform Bills, First and Second, 30–1, 86
religion, 10; church schools, 41; Protestant and Catholic in Ireland, 45; and emigration, 47; in Canada, 50
reservations, *see* Indians
Reuter, Paul, news man, **12**
Rhodes, Cecil, 82, 84, **84**
Rhodesia, 82, **83**, 84

rich, the, *see* ruling classes
Richmond, America, 65, 70, 74
roads, 16, **17**, 52
Rockefeller, John D., oil magnate, 81
Romilly, Samuel, reformer, 38–9
Rossetti, Dante Gabriel, 22, 29
"rotten boroughs", 30–1, **31**
ruling classes, 4–5, 4, 41; in India, 52, **52**; in United States, 61, **62**
Russia, 4, 54–5, 81, 86
Ryder, Albert, artist, 28

sail, *see* ships
St Peter's Field, *see* Peterloo
Sand Creek massacre, 78
Santa Fé Trail, 59
Saxe-Coburg, house of, 5
Scotland, 36, 40
Scott, Dred, American slave, 64
Scott, Gilbert, architect, 20
Scott, Sir Walter, novelist, 42, 86
science, 3, *see also* zoology, inventions
servants, 10–11, **10–11**
settlers, in Australia and New Zealand, 48–9, **48–9**, *see also* emigration
Shaftesbury, Earl of, 34, **34**, 41
Shaw, Bernard, dramatist, 14
Shenandoah Valley, 70, 74
ships; clippers, **7**, 47, 56, **56**; iron, 20, 56–7; prison hulks, **46–7**, 47; riverboats, **57**, **61**, 72; steam, 2, 20, 24, 47, 56–7, **56–7**; steel, 12, 20; warships, 68–9, **68–9**, 72–3, **72–3**; *see also* emigration
Sikhs, 6, 53, **53**
Simpson, James, inventor, 36
Singapore, 6, **7**
Sitting Bull, Indian chief, 79
slavery, 51, 58, 60–4, **61–3**, 70
Smuts, Jan, S. African statesman, 85
Socialism, 32
soldiers; American, 66–7, **66–7**, 70–1; British, 54–5, **54–5**, 82–3; Canadian, 50
Solomon, Joseph, artist, **11**
South Africa, 26, 84–5, **84–5**
South, the, *see* American Civil War, slavery
South America, 20, 59–60, 81
Spain, 81, 83
Speenhamland, system of poor relief, 25
sport, 3, 14–15, **15**
stamps, **13**, 51, 86
Stanley, Henry, explorer, 82
steam; turbine, 20; *see also* agriculture, aircraft, industry, railways, ships, trains
steel; in buildings, **21**; *see also* industry, ships
Stephenson, George and Robert, 8, 20, 86
Stowe, Harriet Beecher, 63, **63**
Sturt, Charles, explorer, 48
submarine, 12
Sudan, the, **7**, 82–3
Suez Canal, 31, 56, 82, 86
Sullivan, Louis, architect, 21
Swann, Joseph, inventor, 13

Tasmania, **48**, 49
telegraph, **12**, 43, 80
Tel-el-Kebir, 83
telephone, 12–13, 80
Tennyson, Alfred Lord, poet, 86
Terry, Ellen, actress, 14
Texas, 58–9, **58**, 65, 76
Thackeray, William Makepeace, novelist, 42, **42**, 86
theatre, 14, **15**
Thomas, Sidney Gilchrist, inventor, 20
Tillet, Ben, trade unionist, 32
Times, the, 37, 43, **43**, 55

tobacco, 60, **63**
Tolpuddle Martyrs, the, 32, 86
Tory Party, 30–1
tourism, **14**
toys, **10**, 12, 40, **41**
trade, 3; decline after war, 4; in British Empire, 6, 7, **7**; in Britain, 18–19; in Europe, United States, 18, 24, **24**
trade unions, 31–3, **32–3**, 80
trains, *see* railways
transport, 2–3, 12, 16–17, **16–17**, *see also* bicycle, motor car, motor cycle, railways, ships
transportation, to colonies, 32, 46–7, **46–7**
Transvaal, 82, 84–5, **84**
Trollope, Anthony, novelist, 42, 86
Turkey, 54, **54**, 86
Turner, J. M., artist, 28, **28**, 86
typewriter, 12
Twain, Mark, novelist, 3, 42, **42**

Ulundi, battle of, 82
Uitlanders, 84
Uncle Tom's Cabin, 683
Union, the, *see* American Civil War
Union Pacific Railway, 61
United States of America, 3; agriculture, 2, 24, 60–1, **61**, 72, 79, 80; architecture, **21**, 51, 67, **79**; railways, **9**, 60–1, 51, **61**, 67, **79**, 80–1, **81**; trade, 18, 80; formation of the Union, 58–9, **58–9**; war with Mexico, 58–9, **59**; the West, 58, 60, 62; the South, 60–3, **62–3**; industry, 62, **64**, 80–1; population, 80, **80**; overseas empire, 80–1, **81**; war with Spain, 81, **81**; *see also* American Civil War, cowboys, Indians, slavery, Wild West

vacuum-cleaner, invention of, 12
Vanderbilt, Cornelius, railwayman, 81
Vicksburg, battle of, 66, 70, 74
Victoria, Queen of England, 5, **11**, **55**, 85–6; succession of, 5; Empress of India, 31, 52
Virginia, 63, 66, 74
Virginia, the (formerly the *Merrimack*), 68, **68–9**, 73

wages, 24–5, 34–5, 40
weapons, 12; in India, 53; in Crimea, **54–5**; in America, **64**, 67, 69, **70**; in Wild West, 76–7, **76**; in South Africa, 85, **85**
Webb, Philip, architect, 21–3
Wellesley, Lord, 52
Wellington, Duke of, British statesman, 4–5, 30
Whig Party, 30
Whitney, Eli, inventor, 60
Whitworth, Joseph, inventor, 20
Wild West, the, 76–7, **76–7**
Wilde, Oscar, dramatist, 14
William IV, king of England, 5, 86
Wills, William, explorer, 48
wireless, *see* radio
Wolseley, Sir Garnet, 83
women, social position of, 10, **14–15**, 39, **39**, *see also* Factory Act, factories
working class, 30–3, **32**, 34–5, **34–5**, *see also* labour, industry, poverty
Wounded Knee, battle of, 78
Wright, Joseph, artist, **19**
writers and literature, 3, 34, 42, **42**

X-rays, 12

Zambezi, River, 82
zoology, 26–7, **27**
Zulus, 82, **82**, 84

DOMINION of CANADA

UNITED KINGDOM

Gibraltar

Bermudas

Bahama Is.

Jamaica

Leeward Is.

Windward Is.

GAMBIA

NIGER

BRITISH HONDURAS

Trinidad

SIERRA LEONE

BRITISH GUIANA

GOLD COAST

Ascension

St. Helena

Pitcairn I.

Tristan da Cunha

Falkland Is.